PRAISE

This book describes a theological [...] [...]ance of throughout the life of Marcus [...] [...]ad and Gray. His music has always been d[...] [...] to Jesus, who is the one who op[...] [...] way into God's presence (John 14:6). As a serious student of Scripture, he ponders the truth of God's Word and discovers the magnitude of God's grace in Jesus in ways he never expected. Grace is given in spite of our own failures, in tangible ways that speak to souls again and again. Life is now lived as one who has been washed, fed, and enlightened with the gifts of Jesus every day. I encourage you to walk with Marcus through his spiritual pilgrimage of discovery.

— **Pastor Dave Haara**, Family of Christ Lutheran Church, Tampa, Florida

For evidence that Lutheranism is the kind of Christianity that has the most relevance today, read FLAME's *Extra Nos*. With a rapper's mastery of language, he offers vivid and rapturous explanations of the Word and the Sacraments and the Gospel of Christ that they convey. And he offers the best refutation of Reformed theology I have ever come across—not just by argument but by experience.

— **Gene Edward Veith**, author of *Spirituality of the Cross*

In the front row, seriously tuned-in, and furiously taking notes but saying very little. Such are my classroom memories of Marcus. And then he opened his mouth, and *Extra Nos* came out. It is a delight to read the account of God's work in the life of one of His servants. And it is powerfully encouraging to read a brother in Christ declare with confidence and clarity the truth of God with fitting conviction. All those who have ever

— **Rev. Dr. Joel Biermann**, professor of systematic theology, Concordia Seminary, St. Louis

FLAME is a consummate student of theology. He embodies the virtue of "in essentials, unity; in non-essentials, liberty; and in all things, charity." This book is a winsome and insightful description of not only what he believes but also how he ended up where he is in his faith journey. You'll find encouragement in these pages. I know I did.

— **Dr. Daniel DeWitt**, senior fellow, Southwest Baptist University, Bolivar, Missouri; executive director of the Center for Worldview and Culture

Christian singer-songwriter FLAME tells the honest story of his humbling journey from the crushing burden of seeking God's grace in his heart and holiness to the liberating joy of receiving God's grace through Christ's gifts of absolution, Baptism, and the Lord's Supper. Through his own story, FLAME calls us all to die to our attempts at searching "inside of us" for the justification of our lives in order to be made alive in Christ through God's gracious work of justification and forgiveness "outside of us" (EXTRA NOS!) and "for us." A must-read for every Lutheran, and every Christian!

— **Rev. Dr. Leopoldo A. Sánchez**, professor of systematic theology, director of the Center for Hispanic Studies, Werner R. H. Krause Professor of Hispanic Ministries, Concordia Seminary, St. Louis

FLAME grew up in St. Louis, Missouri. He and his parents didn't reject the Lutheran Confessions; they had never heard of them. He explored Pentecostalism and Calvinism, but they left him still thirsty. A two-year immersion at Concordia Seminary introduced him to the pure Gospel. His songs now encourage others to believe that "Christ is for YOU." His confessional themes and cutting-edge production contribute to the "mutual conversation and consolation of brothers and sisters." Whether you've heard him or only heard about him, get to know your brother who takes the Lutheran symbols to the streets with lyrical flair and solid confessional content. If you don't know, now you know!

— **Rev. Delwyn X. Campbell**, LCMS national missionary deployed to Gary, Indiana

FLAME shows his theological prowess as he honestly and authentically shares his journey into Lutheranism and how that influences the Lutheran doctrine he writes into rap music. Through his story, FLAME recounts the beautifully persistent work of the Holy Spirit to open his eyes to God's truth, while also sharing how he defends Lutheran thought against other denominations. Whether you're familiar with FLAME's creative work or not, his story is a marvelous example of how we can similarly crave God's Word and a deeper knowledge and understanding of Lutheran doctrine in order to love God and serve our neighbor.

— **Sarah Gulseth**, digital media specialist, KFUO Radio

This book helps Lutherans understand the treasure that we have in our theology. FLAME combines his moving personal journey with a clear exposition of the Lutheran faith. And then he takes it one step further as he follows in the footsteps of Martin Luther by using music to teach the faith. Luther didn't think about using rap music, but he would have if he had known about it!

— **Dr. David R. Maxwell**, professor of systematic theology, Concordia Seminary, St. Louis

Marcus (FLAME) invites us into his struggle of living the Christian life by trying to balance and understand it through one of the many wonderful Lutheran distinctions, the two kinds of righteousness—in other words, learning the distinction between passive and active righteousness. I, too, found this joy, coming late to the Lutheran table, by discovering the beauty of Baptism, forgiveness, and reconciliation in a similar fashion. At one point, Marcus speaks of his complex, diverse, curious, and confusing self, which seeks to find the pure mercy, grace, peace, and love of Christ. He discovers these have always been there and found freely outside himself—extra nos—in Christ.

— **Dr. Beth Hoeltke**, director of the Graduate School, Concordia Seminary, St. Louis

Extra Nos is FLAME's story about how Jesus' promise that "you shall know the truth, and the truth shall make you free" has been fulfilled in his own life and art. It is a story of being freed from uncertainty, confusion, and doubts as he discovered God's grace in Christ outside himself. *Extra Nos* is at once personal and accessible, honest and generous, fresh and faithful, unorthodox and confessional.

— **Dr. Joel P. Okamoto**, Waldemar and Mary Griesbach Professor of Systematic Theology, Concordia Seminary, St. Louis

FLA
ME

EXTRA
NOS

DISCOVERING
GRACE OUTSIDE
MYSELF

Published by Concordia Publishing House

3558 S. Jefferson Avenue, St. Louis, MO 63118-3968

1-800-325-3040 • cph.org

Copyright © 2023 Marcus "FLAME" Gray

All rights reserved. No part of this publication may be reproduced, stored in a retrieval system, or transmitted, in any form or by any means, electronic, mechanical, photocopying, recording, or otherwise, without the prior written permission of Concordia Publishing House.

Scripture quotations are from the ESV® Bible (The Holy Bible, English Standard Version®), copyright © 2001 by Crossway, a publishing ministry of Good News Publishers. Used by permission. All rights reserved.

The quotations from the Lutheran Confessions in this publication are from *Concordia: The Lutheran Confessions*, second edition © 2006 Concordia Publishing House. All rights reserved.

The quotation from *Luther's Works* is from the American Edition, vol. 45 © 1962 by Fortress Press. Used by permission of the publisher.

Quotations from *Has American Christianity Failed?* © 2016 Bryan Wolfmueller. Used by permission.

Quotation from *The Spirituality of the Cross* is from the revised edition © 2010 Concordia Publishing House. All rights reserved.

The quote from *Annotations on the Gospel According to St. John* © 2019 Adolph Spaeth, published by Just and Sinner Publications. Used by permission.

All quoted rap lyrics © FLAME. All rights reserved.

Manufactured in the United States of America

1 2 3 4 5 6 7 8 9 10   32 31 30 29 28 27 26 25 24 23

I DEDICATE THIS BOOK TO

MY DEAREST GRANDMOTHER,

FRANCES JONES, AND MY

BELOVED PARENTS, CAROLYN AND

SAMMIE GRAY. WE SHALL ALL

MEET AGAIN, ONE DAY. IN CHRIST.

CONTENTS

PART I

BEGINNINGS

CHAPTER 1

HOW THE REFORMATION REACHED RAPPERS

Under normal circumstances, there is no earthly reason I can possibly think of that would have made the reformer Martin Luther a topic of conversation at my church home. Imagine a church body filled with 100 percent Black Americans in the heart of the hood and affiliated with the Full Gospel denomination—a mix between Baptist and Pentecostal. In that context, the Reformation simply was not at the top of the list of topics.

As a sixteen-year-old Christian, enjoying life and hanging out with my bros at youth night, I remember my youth pastor making mention of this Martin Luther. He told us Martin Luther King Jr. was named after him. For some reason, that little fact stuck with me. At the time, I wasn't all that interested. I do recall thinking something like, *Oh, that's pretty cool.* If I'm honest, I didn't try to store the information in any particular place in my brain since it had no immediate relevance. Yet for some reason, I retained it.

Later that night, I found myself wondering about the guy Martin Luther King Jr. was named after. I remember my youth pastor saying he was a German man. I thought, *Martin Luther is an African American name. How did a German man get such an African American name?* The inquiry of a sixteen-year-old. **It wasn't until** five years later that the reformer Martin Luther would again become the subject of conversation.

Oh, did I mention that I'm a Christian rapper? After almost losing my life in a tragic car accident as a teenager, I committed my way to the Lord afresh. What happened was this: while I was leaving orientation at a new school, the car I was riding in with a friend and his mom was hit by an eighteen-wheeler carrying fuel. We were spinning in a 360 down the highway at about sixty-five miles per hour. Eventually, there was a twelve-car pileup. We hit the left shoulder of the highway, and the car flipped over. I had to do physical therapy for over a year. It was a pivotal moment in my faith. Although I was raised as a Christian and was baptized around four or five years old, I hadn't laid hold of my faith in a deep or committed way yet. We'll discuss later in the book how I now view my Baptism, but for now, let's think of my dramatic experience as a "conversion." After my "conversion" at sixteen, I gave up my mainstream rap aspirations and committed my music and my content to strictly Christian doctrine.

CHRISTIAN RAP

As a teenager, I thought I invented good Christian rap—that I alone originated this new and innovative genre of music. Now, I was exposed to some Christian rap as a kid. A local ministry once gathered all the addresses in my inner-city project building and mailed us all a Gospel rap cassette tape. I'll never forget it. On the cover art was plastered two guys and the group name. I thought, *Well, a church sent it to us. At least I can "do God a solid" and listen to it.* There was only one song on the tape. I put the cassette in my Walkman. I confess it was one of the worst songs my ears had ever been exposed to. In the spirit of Saul before his conversion, I took it upon myself to do God's work by leaving the tape outside in the scorching heat so that it could melt over time under the blazing sun. Surely God was pleased! Yet I gave the guys credit for not cursing.

Fast forward to my "conversion" experience at age 16, mentioned earlier. Now that I was locked in and serious about my faith unlike ever before, I knew I could no longer listen to the kind of rap music I was accustomed to. I figured that if I'd be embarrassed to ride around in my car listening to a song that Jesus couldn't rap along with me, then maybe I shouldn't be listening to it. Off to the Christian bookstore I went! A friend of mine who was not a Christian told me about a rap group he saw on MTV that was rapping about Jesus. He mentioned that their name was The Cross Movement. I made a mental note.

Heading into the bookstore, I was excited to make a large purchase of new rap music that did not offend women or celebrate crime and that ultimately was all about Jesus. I opened the store doors and went straight to the hip hop section. I was overwhelmed. There were so many CDs. So many artists. I had no idea. I grabbed a handful of CDs and placed them one by one in the CD player for sampling. I put the headphones over my ears and began listening. Album after album, I found artists from all over the US who had a similar story to me and who had, too, committed their lives and music to Jesus at a young age. I was in paradise!

I wasn't at the bookstore alone. A good friend of mine who went by the name of JR was with me. He brought a tape over to my listening section and tapped my shoulder to get my attention. My eyes were closed, as I had blissfully drifted into the music and the message. I took the headphones off and raised my eyebrows as if to say, "Uh huh, what's up?" He showed me the cassette.

"Aren't these those dudes you told me about?" he asked.

I grabbed the tape, exclaiming, "Yeah! This is them!"

I quickly opened the jewel case, snapped the tape in the deck, and pressed play. **A symphony of strings, the traditional hip hop "boom bap" drum cadence, and the finest of East Coast–laden rap performance jumped out of the album and into my soul.** I was elated. I called to my friend from across the store. The store manager heard me first and asked if I could use my inside voice. I obliged. My friend walked back over, and I told him, "Bro, you have to listen to this!" He put the headphones on and had a similar reaction. We were both overwhelmingly inspired.

Needless to say, I made the purchase and became an instant fan of Cross Movement. From that point on, I obsessed over them. This new invention called the internet had just become popular, and I found out that they occupied a space there called a website. Their site contained not only an artist page but also a ministry page. They had taken mission trips to reservations to share the Gospel. They shared daily devotionals, encouraging their supporters to be bold in their faith and pure in their lives. Instantly, in my heart, I esteemed them as mentors, heroes of the faith.

The timing couldn't have been better. I, too, was active in my local church—sharing my Gospel rap publicly at youth night, performing and speaking in prisons and juvenile detention centers, doing street evangelism, and the like. I used Cross Movement's music as the soundtrack to my rap ministry. I visited their website regularly and kept close tabs on their whereabouts. When new music was releasing. What new devotionals and articles were posted. One day, I stumbled upon their tour schedule. I noticed that they were coming to a city near St. Louis: Chicago. By this point, I was a fan two or three years in. I checked the date on their Chicago event to see if it had already passed. I thought for sure that we missed them and that the date simply hadn't been removed from the website yet.

Just to be sure, I decided to double-check. Wait! What? The date was upcoming? You mean these complete strangers whom I had grown to admire profoundly as distant mentors in the faith were coming to the Midwest? They were based all the way in Philadelphia. What business did they have near my hometown? Immediately, I went to a website called MapQuest to see how far Chicago was from St. Louis. (There was no such thing as GPS at the time unless you were some high-ranking military spy.) I was just a teen from the inner city who loved Jesus and was loved by Him. And Jesus just placed my favorite rap group in my path.

I called my friends instantly and shared the good news. They, too, were in disbelief and excited about the possibility of meeting these guys. I began planning the trip. **Eventually, the date rolled around, and it was time to hit the road.** In my truck were three of my close friends who were just as ecstatic about what was ahead of us. It was only my second road trip. For the other one, the same group of guys and I had driven to a conference to hear our favorite preachers. This time, we were heading to see our favorite Christian rap group.

We were in my silver Ford F150 having the time of our lives, and about three hours in, we realized we maybe missed an exit. All we had was a printout of directions from MapQuest. Trying to figure out east from west, I suppose we missed an exit or two. We were freaking out! What if we missed the concert? What if the guys went up first and we missed the chance to see them perform? Panic filled the truck cabin. We did the next best thing: we pulled over to a gas station and asked for directions. A kind gentleman gave us clear directions to get back on track, and we were off.

Finally, we made it. Albeit late, but we made it nonetheless. We pulled up to the church venue and found a great parking spot. That lifted our spirits. Approaching the door, we were all nervous and excited at the same time. As we each pulled out our concert fare, we heard rap music in the distance. I remember thinking, "Wow, I never knew Christian rappers have concerts." As we made our way into the crowd, to our pleasant surprise, Cross Movement had just taken the stage. The night couldn't get any better. They began performing one of my favorite songs of theirs, and everyone knew the lyrics, word for word. Like we did.

We thought we were the only people who were superfans. We were wrong. A room full of teenage guys and girls shouted deep theological rap lyrics at the top of their lungs. It was unbelievable; it was like we all knew one another. Complete strangers standing side by side, quoting Christian rap lyrics back and forth to one another while Cross Movement was right there on stage. In

Luke 2:28–31, Simeon beheld baby Jesus and concluded, "Okay, I can depart and go to heaven now." While our experience was *not* holding the baby Jesus, we, too, felt a sense of awe and gratitude for this encounter God had given us.

A PIVOTAL MOMENT

As if things couldn't get any better, after their last song, Cross Movement announced that they'd be hanging out afterward to take pictures and sign autographs. It was too much—we were overwhelmed. We made our way to their merchandise table, and there they were. Well, most of them. Out of five artists total, two hadn't made it out yet. Nervously, my friends and I approached their table and spoke to them. One artist in particular, The Tonic, politely asked us where we were from.

"St. Louis, Missouri."

"St. Louis? Where is that?"

We were like, "Wow, we're not even on the map." We all laughed.

One of my bros whispered to me, "Hey you should go give them one of your demos."

A demo is an album that you prepare for a record label. That was the last thing on my mind at the time. I was simply awestruck to be that close to the artist I had admired and studied from afar for years. I responded to my friend that I didn't want to come across like I wanted something from them. I didn't want to be *that guy*. My personality is not prone to being an opportunist.

Unbeknownst to me, a few of the guys ran to my truck and grabbed a few of my CDs. They flew back into the building, short of breath, and handed me a copy. Awkward. Yet I was happy that my bros were looking out for me. I asked The Tonic if he would mind if I gave him one of my demos.

"Not at all," he said.

What manner of miracle was this? How is it that Cross Movement now had a *FLAME CD*? There was no such thing as a selfie back then, and even with a truck full of teenagers, everyone forgot to bring a disposable camera. The moment was too surreal to interrupt for picture-taking anyway.

As you can imagine, we talked about the concert and meeting these giants in the Christian rap genre all the way back to St. Louis. **Still in concert mode, we played their music at max volume, rapping all the lyrics and enjoying the fellowship.**

One of my friends blurted out, "Wouldn't it be crazy if Cross Movement was listening to your CD right now?"

I was like, "Wow, I can't even imagine!"

"What song do you picture them liking the most?" someone else asked.

We all took turns guessing which song would resonate with which member of the group. I was still in disbelief and not taking the possibility to heart. I knew record labels rarely listen to demos and those CDs normally become coasters for coffee or Frisbees for kids.

CHAPTER 2

A DREAM COME TRUE

This next part of the story will blow your mind. Seriously—I could not make this stuff up if I wanted to. After the road trip to Chicago, we eventually settled back into the regular course of things. Perhaps a week or so into the mundane, during a good night's rest and the sweet rewards of REM sleep, I fell into a dream. In the dream, I was also sleeping. (That's how good the sleep was!) I was in my sleep, sleeping. Not only that but in my dream I was asleep dreaming. Did you get that? While actually sleeping in real life, having a dream, my dream was of me asleep dreaming. In the dream, I was awakened by a call from Cross Movement. I looked at the caller ID screen and saw their logo. In the dream, I woke up flustered and in a panic. I nervously cleared my throat to answer the phone so as to appear awake. All of this was in my dream.

Here comes the mind-bending part of the story. What actually woke me up from my dream that Cross Movement was calling me was an actual call from Cross Movement! In real life, my exact dream happened at the same time. I woke up and saw their name on my caller ID. I was utterly floored. I felt a little like Paul in 2 Corinthians 12:2, when he wasn't sure if he was in the body or out of the body.

How was this possible? I had no time to think. I didn't want to miss the call, so I quickly cleared my throat and picked up the phone.

"Hello," I said in a mildly raspy voice.

"May I speak to FLAME?" someone asked.

"Hey, this is me, FLAME!"

This someone—the CEO of Cross Movement—told me how much the group liked my album and that they'd be interested in building a relationship over the phone. We entertained meeting regularly on a call to have Bible studies and to get to know one another. I was 100 percent okay with that and told them that I'd be delighted to do so.

We talked for at least thirty minutes, which felt a lot longer (but I wasn't complaining). After we got off the phone, I took a moment to take it all in. I remember thanking God for arranging these events. Eventually, I got around to calling my bros who took the road trip with me. They, too, were awestruck. As time passed, Cross Movement made good on their word. We would regularly talk on the phone about life, the Scriptures, culture, art, music, and the music industry. **The bond we were establishing was deepening and rewarding.**

I would share with them stories of how we were impacting our community using rap music, and they would share war stories from being in the music business as Christian rap artists. It was a powerful time of iron sharpening iron. We were moving from strangers to acquaintances to friends. This continued for a few years. I honestly was happy with just having them as friends. Just knowing I had access to the guys that inspired me from a distance was satisfying in and of itself. Yet it appeared God had more in mind. Much more.

THE INVITATION

As we were about to end a call one day, the CEO of Cross Movement began to tell me that they were in the process of expanding their record label. He talked about his desire to bring other acts to the company so that people would know it wasn't about them but about what Jesus was doing all over the world using rap music. Not simply rap music but rap artists from the urban and inner-city contexts who would yield their talents to the Lordship of Jesus Christ intentionally as urban missionaries.

I fell in love with the vision he was presenting. I shared with him that I thought it was a great idea. This turned into an invitation to be a part of this new development. He asked me if I would like to be a part of their record label. With no hesitation, I told him that I'd be more than honored to be under the same label imprint as Cross Movement. I did not see that coming. I was completely shocked and caught off guard.

This invitation spoke to me deeply. It felt like the most natural progression to everything that was on my mind and heart to do with my rap music. I was already rapping locally and seeing great results—God was saving and encouraging people through Gospel witness in my city. **This opportunity only made sense, and I was elated to step into the unknown to see what all God had in store.** As if that wasn't enough, this Philadelphia native also mentioned that they were planning a tour. The goal was to hit thirty cities in two months. He asked if I'd be interested in being a part of it. My answer was an emphatic *yes*! Just the thought of being in the same air space as the group for two months sounded like utter bliss. As we exited the conversation, we prayed and asked God to bless our plans and to make our path straight. I could not wait to call my friend and producer and share the good news with him; Cross Movement wanted both of us to be a part of the label and pending tour.

I was still living with my parents, so it was only right to consult with them first. They asked me all the necessary parental questions and eventually gave me the green light. I was encouraged to have their support to pursue what I believed God was empowering me to do as a young adult. Next, I felt it necessary to discuss the matter with my pastor. I certainly wanted his blessing as well, as I was extremely active in my local church and outreach activities. I just knew he would be happy for us—two of his prime young adult leaders were going on to tour and to do inner-city missionary work, using our music and rap talents.

A DIFFICULT CONVERSATION

I scheduled the meeting to chat with my pastor about this amazing opportunity, and he obliged. Eventually, the scheduled time rolled around. As I pulled into the church parking lot, I couldn't help but wonder how my pastor would respond. I stepped into his office, and he appeared to be in good spirits. He offered me a seat and asked how I was doing. I told him I was doing exceptionally well. In fact, I was doing so well that I decided to schedule the current meeting to talk about how well things were going.

I gave him a thorough recap of all the recent events that led up to our time that day. The road trip. Meeting Cross Movement in person. Giving them my demo. The dream. The phone call. The opportunity to be on their record label and to tour with them. As I brought my entire monologue in for a landing, his face sort of went blank. He sat there in stunned silence. Was this a pause for dramatic effect? Was this the kind of overwhelming joy that causes a person to be at a loss for words? I was confused. I decided to break the silence.

"I just wanted to let you know about these things so you wouldn't think we were leaving the church for good or anything like that."

"This is the best church in the world. There is no better place for you all to go," he replied.

This shocking response left me perplexed.

In all fairness, this was my first awkward experience with my pastor. Otherwise, I—and many others—found him to be a most admirable gentleman worthy of following, which made his response all the more puzzling. Needless to say, the meeting did not go well. At all.

I spoke with my youth pastor about the experience. He encouraged us and told us to not be distracted. We prayed together, as he asked the Lord to strengthen our hearts and to give us a posture of forgiveness, knowing that we all fall short. He then assured us that he would speak to the head pastor on our behalf and vouch for our character and motivations. This brought us much comfort and courage, knowing that we had the blessing of our youth pastor. We were determined to not let that experience rob us of the excitement of the opportunity. Off we went to prepare for two months away from home. **A feat neither of us had ever undertaken.**

PART II

THE START
OF A JOURNEY

CHAPTER 3

THE JOURNEY BEGINS

The time for the tour arrived. My bags were packed and I was ready to take a flight to New York, of all places. Up until that point, I had never been on an airplane before. In fact, the furthest I'd ever been away from home was that trip to Chicago. To go from that meager travel experience to New York City was both frightening and exciting. The most nerve-wracking part was all the steps it took to get to the plane. Finding the correct terminal, learning how to use the kiosk, going through security, keeping up with bag tags, monitoring the screens for updated boarding information, baggage claim, and curbside pickup all proved to be overwhelming. Not to mention, people from New York City weren't all too social. Nonetheless, I did find that the actual flight was calming and pretty fun. I loved every minute in the sky. I just gazed at God's creation from a crushing altitude of forty thousand feet. I couldn't help but admire human ingenuity and the advent of air travel. God is certainly kind to His human creatures in how He distributes intelligence and creativity.

Finally, we arrived at the starting point for the tour and saw the entire team. It was incredible! We not only saw the group members again but also the people that work behind the scenes to make everything flow and function smoothly. **It felt like home,**

a second family. As we boarded the tour bus, loaded our luggage in the undercarriage, and claimed our bunk, we all began to get acquainted with one another. People were unpacking video game consoles and pulling out their favorite movies and music-production equipment. I was loving it!

While on the road, one of the artists from the beloved group asked my homie and me, "Are you Calvinist or Arminian?"

To which I responded, "Huh? Can you say that again?"

"Are you a Calvinist or an Arminian?" he repeated.

"I'm not sure what you're asking," I replied.

He went on to give a short but sufficient explanation of the two terms in use. After hearing him out, I stated, "Oh, I simply follow Jesus."

It kind of felt like I was being asked which gang I was in—to which I remained neutral. When all else fails, follow Jesus. The artist asserted that every Christian was either a Calvinist or an Arminian regardless of whether they were aware of it.

I had never thought about my faith in either of those terms. In fact, I had never heard of either of the gentlemen these two sides were named after. I was learning that I needed to take them seriously and pick a side. Plus, from the look of things, it seemed like Calvin was the "correct" choice. Obviously, it was not an overnight decision. Far from it. For two months straight, city after city, state after state, **we had weighty theological discussions, Bible studies, and quiet time for reflection.** I was careful to not make any verbal commitments to either theological camp. I simply wanted to ask as many questions as I could possibly think of and to gather as much information and understanding as I could about the two positions. Much was at stake.

Another topic of discussion that kept rising to the surface was the Charismatic and Word of Faith denominations, of which I was a part at the time. This was particularly important to me and caused me to perk up because it was the origin of my Christian experience—not to mention the experience of the majority of the Christians I had known up to that point. Martin Luther came up a little too, but I still wouldn't hear much about him until much later.

A LOOK BACK TO MOVE FORWARD

I credit Frances Jones, my dear grandmother whom I called "Mother," in a particularly special way for leading me to Jesus. Both she and my beloved mom, Carolyn Gray, impressed upon me the endless wonder of the triune God. I was hooked. My young imagination ran wild with amazement at things like heaven, angels, a talking donkey, people walking on water, miraculous healings, and the mysterious nature of God Himself.

While these exciting realities were ever present in my Christian circle, so was the poisonous nature of many unhealthy teachings. Long before I learned about the Latin phrase *extra nos*, which means "outside of us," I was coached into mastering God's voice from within. This was commonplace in the church culture I was from. I'll never forget a sermon series someone gave my mom titled "How to Hear God's Voice." It was a total of four cassette tapes, two on each side of a plastic folding case. The cover art was a headshot of a pastor suspended in the clouds. He looked like a nice guy, so I figured he had to know what he was talking about.

Yep, the reasoning of a sixteen-year-old.

I quietly took the sermon series to my room, excited to master the art of hearing what God was saying to me from within. The pastor promised to teach you not only how to hear directly from God but also how to discern if the inner voice you were hearing was from your own flesh or Satan and his demons.

The pastor warned, "You might think it's God talking to you because the voice is saying things you want, but that could be your flesh tricking you. Or worse, the devil using your desires to trap you. 'Take that job,' the voice says. 'It's near your home and has great pay. It's perfect!' However, that could be Satan using your own voice in your mind and your desires to entangle you in a job that will drain you of joy."

I thought to myself, *Oh no! There are at least three different voices I need to listen out for? This is going to be harder than I thought.* I was not happy but discouraged.

Nonetheless, if this was what it meant to be a Christian, then I wanted it. I desired to please God. I longed for a personal word from Him, a word affirming His approval of me and my spiritual maturity, demonstrated by regularly receiving tailored messages from Him. I wanted messages of assurance and specific instructions on how to serve those around me. With spontaneity. I confess, I only made it through a tape and a half of the sermon series. The pastor kept repeating the same things, only said in different ways. I lost interest and figured I had the gist.

However, before I went to bed that night, I prayed an earnest prayer that went something like this: "Dear Father, in the name of

Jesus, thank You for saving me from my sin. I really want to do Your work and have an impact on my generation. Please help me hear Your voice and know when You are speaking to me. Please help me discern whether or not it's You talking to me, my sinful flesh, or the devil and his imps. I can't tell sometimes. What if the devil or my flesh tells me to do a thing and I mistakenly think it was from You? I don't want to disappoint You, Lord. Please make Your voice clear to me. In Jesus' name. Amen." I went to sleep.

This was a heavy burden to carry. Much was at stake. The task of knowing how to hear from God was supposed to demonstrate that you were growing spiritually and that God was pleased with you, that He could trust you with special tasks and responsibilities. Indeed, it was customary for me to regularly hear people say things like "God told me" or "I heard God say." Nothing in my immediate environment or context would have caused me to see this as strange or excessive. After all, in the Bible, God spoke to people audibly and in dreams.

What complicated the task even more was that there were times when the people who made claims to have heard from heaven stated things that proved true. But that wasn't my most pressing concern. The most pressing thing was noticing how often people would hear wrongly. For example, a person who got it right once was now getting it wrong. Those examples of people stuck with me. I could not dismiss that observation: they got it wrong. They claimed God said something that did not come to pass or that contradicted Scripture. I did not want to be like them. Therefore, I thought to myself, *I must master this art of hearing from my heavenly Father.*

LOSS OF ASSURANCE

What better way to get good at something than to practice? And after practice comes the test. Aching to know if my spiritual growth was up to par, I decided to try my hand at discerning God's voice from within. This led to countless expressions of "stepping out in faith," ranging from putting myself in dangerous situations because "God told me to" to simple spontaneous acts of kindness. I vowed to myself and to God that nothing "He would tell me to do" would be off-limits. If He trusted me with the task, then that meant He would be with me during it.

To be sure, there is nothing wrong with living the Christian life with an ever-ready attitude of spontaneity for good works. That, indeed, is right and good. However, the lines can become blurred when one has attached his or her spiritual aptitude toward the supernatural to God's pleasure or displeasure. **In other words, if I believe the ability to distinguish God's voice means that God is more pleased with me than He already is simply because I am a forgiven sinner in Christ, then I have misplaced the true biblical basis for God's pleasure toward His children.** God's pleasure is found in Christ, by faith.

I am a witness of this firsthand. As mentioned, during the earlier stages of my Christian journey, I was a member of a tradition that was more than friendly toward Charismatic teachings. During a Wednesday night Bible study, a guest preacher was teaching on Spirit Baptism, although then I would not have understood it by that term. Spirit Baptism is the teaching that Christians must receive a second baptism or a "second blessing" after becoming a Christian. It is a superior baptism over water Baptism. Supporters of this teaching use John the Baptist's words in Matthew 3:11:

> I baptize you with water for repentance, but He
> who is coming after me is mightier than I, whose
> sandals I am not worthy to carry. He will baptize
> you with the Holy Spirit and fire.

These words are used incorrectly to mean that water Baptism is good but that the true power for the Christian life lies in the better "Spirit Baptism" that must be expressed by speaking in tongues. If one had not received the Holy Spirit, evidenced by speaking in tongues, then they were living beneath the true Christian experience, perhaps even resisting God or not deemed by Him to be worthy. Maybe there is secret sin in the person's life, or maybe the person has little faith and isn't trusting God enough.

The guest preacher was explaining to a room of about sixty people that we may be experiencing sickness or trouble in our home life or work life, even unanswered prayer, due to this missing component God desired for us to have. Then, as he was mid-sentence, the lights in the sanctuary went out. A complete blackout. **An immediate silence took over the room as all stood shocked and confused.** The lead pastor shouted in a loud voice, "It's okay, it's okay. The bills have been paid and the circuit breaker will kick on in a minute."

While waiting for the lights to come back on, the guest speaker decided to redeem the moment. He exclaimed that God decided to shut the lights off because He knew many in the room were overly concerned about those sitting around them. For that reason, His Holy Spirit could not "move" in the room. He went on to say we should see the darkness as a blessing and the perfect environment to practice speaking in tongues.

From there on, he instructed us to repeatedly say the word *hallelujah*.

"Faster, faster," he shouted. "Let the Holy Spirit take control!"

As the loud, repetitive cries of *hallelujah* consumed the room, I turned to my friend and said, "Man, this is getting weird." He nodded his head in agreement but was at a loss for words.

I turned to him again and whispered, "Bro, I'm about to leave."

He giggled and whispered back, "Nah, man, stay, maybe God is doing something." To appease him and with a hint of curiosity, I decided to stay.

Suddenly, the lights came back on, and the room erupted with shouts of praise. The visiting speaker then asked, "How many people received the gift of the Spirit evidenced in tongues?" The majority of people in the room raised their hands. I, on the other hand, experienced nothing but anxiety, fear, and condemnation. Why didn't God pick me? Why didn't the Holy Spirit take control of me like He did the others? Was I not sincere enough? I felt forgotten and unworthy.

The guest speaker offered to stay a while longer after service to help anyone who did not receive the gift. Apparently, I wasn't the only one "the Holy Spirit passed over." At least three others approached the guest seeking this "second blessing." I was first in line. He called me forward and assured me that tonight was my night. "Close your eyes," he said. "Repeat *hallelujah* really fast, and then utter a few syllables. Let the Holy Spirit control your speech."

A few of my comrades stood by laughing in the distance. I tried to ignore them and to earnestly focus on God. I really wanted all He had for me.

As I began to spout out random gibberish that sounded like what's become known as the gift of tongues, the visiting orator shouted, "That's it; you have the gift!" He then told me to keep practicing and that the Holy Spirit would strengthen me in the gift over time. I walked away not feeling any better. That was it? I just parroted some sounds, and now I have access to top-tier power from heaven? The entire experience was altogether odd. **I left overcome with doubt and despair.** *Oh well*, I thought. *Who knows?*

A RELATABLE EXPERIENCE

As I shared this and other experiences like it with the guys on tour, they heavily expressed that they could relate. They shared with me that many of them had come from that type of background. They cautioned me against extreme expressions of Charismatic and Prosperity-driven preaching and encouraged me to continue to know the Word of God for myself. That way, I could weigh what's being said up against the Scriptures.

On the road, I continued sharing with them the character of the amazing church home where I held membership but also some of the questionable things that concerned me. It appeared that some of the doctrine and many of the practices were moving closer and closer toward some of the extremes that they warned against. Before the tour, I noticed a few shifts, but I was believing the best, knowing that no church is perfect.

I asked, "Are people from the Charismatic Church Calvinist or Arminian?"

The answer I got: "Most likely Arminian."

For our purposes here, it is not important to know a great deal about Arminians and Calvinists. Here are some of the general ideas in contrast. Calvinists believe Jesus did not die for everyone. They are quick to add that Jesus' death was powerful enough to cover everyone's sin if He desired so. Yet it was not His desire to die for all without exception. Arminians believe Jesus did die for all without exception.

Calvinists teach, by and large, that Jesus elected some people for eternal life and some for eternal judgment (hell) to glorify His wrath. Arminians do not believe the Bible teaches that. Calvinists teach that humans are born dead in sin and can do nothing on their own accord to save themselves because our will is in bondage to sin. Arminians believe humans are crippled by sin but are still able to choose God based on their will and intellectual reasoning. Calvinists do not believe a person can lose their salvation. They'd argue that a person who was a "professing Christian" but later walked away from the faith was "never really saved in the first place." Arminians believe a true Christian can decide to leave Christianity and thus forfeit their faith. The truth of the matter is, respectfully, both Calvinists and Arminians can benefit greatly from allowing the Lutheran voice to help explain the missing pieces of both their arguments and conclusions. More to come concerning that later.

Back to the tour bus discussions. Many of the members of the group had either been formally trained in Bible college or seminary or were gifted lay leaders. They provided plausible reasoning for their Calvinistic case. As I was not formally trained and newly exposed to these matters, I was simply processing it all, trying to gauge where I leaned the most after a cursory consideration. There was much more digging to do; I had my work cut out for me.

Inspired by the group, I had already enrolled in Bible college before the tour. As the summer months were approaching an end, the school year was about to begin. For that reason, I had to leave the tour early and head back to St. Louis to start my first semester of Bible college. It was bittersweet. I'd had the most awe-inspiring experience. We were able to bond and share the same stage together. Share a tour bus and the Gospel together. However, I was excited to take all this new information back to my local church and to my college professors to see what they thought about these matters. I was curious if the Bible college I'd enrolled in was a Calvinist institution or an Arminian institution. In a sense, it didn't matter. **I was simply excited to learn and dig into God's Word for myself.** The timing could not have been any better.

CHAPTER 4

TIME FOR SCHOOL

Once I returned home and got settled, I was charged up and ready to learn. I unloaded all these "new" ideas and doctrines on my youth pastor. He was happy to see me so excited about the Word of God, Church history, and about how much I enjoyed the tour. In fact, I journaled daily and had been sure to document how I felt each day and the things I was learning. In addition, I shared as much as people would lend me time for—not only with my youth leader but also with our prayer group. I asked them to pray that God would give me clarity, that He would lead me to the knowledge of the truth. They, too, were happy to see someone from the youth group so "on fire for the Lord."

About a week after the tour, the zeal began to wane. I detected more and more unhealthy things at church that were discussed on tour. Should I leave the church? Why is the pastor asking us who desires to be rich? Why is there an altar call to give hundreds of dollars to the Lord so that He can "bless you ten-, twenty-, and some hundredfold?" Were we Calvinists or Arminians? I didn't want to be hasty and leave the church home that had so richly blessed me. God had given me a gift in that community of believers, and I witnessed Him do so much good in my life and the lives of others. My friends were there with whom the entire spectrum of my social life existed. I was deeply troubled.

I gave myself to endurance and long-suffering. After all, if any group of people deserved it, it was this one. While regularly attending services, Bible studies, and youth nights, I began to innocently ask questions. I thought, *Who better to ask than the clergy?* Respectfully, I just wasn't being given the type of answers and engagement that I received on tour. *Should I reserve my questions for my Bible college professors? Who knows*, I pondered privately.

Attending a Bible study one night, my pastor made a statement. He said, out of what seemed to be nowhere, "A lot of people go to seminary school, but it's really cemetery school. They go in with an empty head and a full heart and come out with a full head and an empty heart." Wow! This felt like a blow to the gut. I wondered if he was talking about me. I mean, I certainly understood his point and can see some validity to it on occasion, but to make a sweeping statement about seminary in general felt a bit rash.

At this point, I was praying without ceasing, asking God for direction. I was considering leaving the church more seriously. I decided to schedule another meeting with my pastor. Although the first one didn't go so well, I still respected him and wanted him to know what I was thinking through and feeling. Again, he obliged. Again, we went back to his office.

"Thanks for meeting with me, Pastor. First, I wanted to ask for your forgiveness," I told him. "After our first meeting, I harbored a bit of anger toward you, and that was not right. Will you forgive me?"

"Yes, of course," he replied.

After a brief while of heavy discussion, it appeared that we weren't getting anywhere. I finally told him that I no longer considered myself a member there for theological reasons. I thanked him for his priceless contribution to my walk as a teenage Christian. I praised his leadership and his trust in me after having made me a young adult deacon.

He understood, and we parted ways amicably. **I felt both relieved and sad at the same time.** Relieved that as a twenty-something, I was following the path I believed God was taking me down. Sad that I was witnessing the closing of a chapter and had no idea what was in front of me. Curious times, for sure.

THEOLOGICAL CRISIS ON CAMPUS

I was living on campus at Bible college and in need of a church home. That was a thing I took seriously and did not want to over-look. However, I had much to consider before joining another body of believers. Now that I had been exposed to Calvinism and it appeared to be faithful to the Bible, I wanted to know more about it. Yet I had no clue what or where a Calvinist church was. I decided not to start there but to simply gather as much as I could about the matter from my classes.

Truthfully, my soul was becoming restless. I was being invaded by fear. I was surely experiencing a theological crisis. My entire life was built around the tenets of my former church home. That's where I learned how to understand God, the Bible, the world around me, and, most important, my own salvation—not to mention the salvation of those I loved.

I was afraid to read my Bible because I didn't want to read my former theological ideas into the text of Scripture. For example, a passage like Isaiah 54:17:

> No weapon that is fashioned against you
> shall succeed.

Coming out of my previous tradition, this passage meant to me that God would not allow harmful attacks to actually damage me. Yet I experienced a few attacks that were "fashioned," and they "succeeded." For that reason, I knew there were gaps in my understanding on how to even approach Bible study and my daily devotional time.

During this tumultuous time, I could not help but wonder about my grandmother. I had not worked through whether being a Calvinist or an Arminian was an essential matter of salvation. To my knowledge, my grandmother had never thought of or talked about Christianity in either of those terms. To be honest, I didn't want to think about it. Before I had a right understanding that my dear grandmother was loved and saved by Jesus and did not need to choose between those two options, I didn't have the emotional wherewithal to think it through.

I knew she loved Jesus deeply and that she had given her life to impacting her family and those around her with the Gospel and acts of sacrifice and kindness. Yet, at the time, I wasn't sure of what all it took to be "saved." I desperately hoped that was enough. It was weighty ponderings like these that caused me to slip into a mild depression. I started skipping class, hanging out just to be social, and failing to complete my homework assignments. I even set things before my eyes that I knew did not honor God or my neighbor. It's safe to say I felt lost. Disoriented, even.

HERMENEUTICS CLASS

As I was getting settled in my dorm room one night, I prayed and asked God to lead me to the passage of Scripture that He wanted me to read. My prayer went something like this: "Dear Father, in the name of Jesus, I want to hear from You. I want You to speak to me and help me understand Your Word. Give me a specific word that You want me to hear during this season of life. In Jesus' name I pray. Amen."

Afterward, I sat in a meditative state of silence, hoping to "hear back from God." Not too long after the prayer, I "heard" a voice in my head say, "Turn to Mark chapter 17, son." I couldn't have been more shocked and excited! *Finally, I'm discerning the voice of God,* I thought. He had spoken directly to me and in a speedy manner. I thanked Him aloud and went rushing through the pages of my Bible. Eventually, I tracked down the Book of Mark.

As I was thumbing through the pages, I turned from Mark chapter 14 to 15 and finally to Mark chapter 16. Yep, that was it. The Book of Mark stops at chapter 16. There is no seventeenth chapter. I was furious! I yelled out loud, "Stop playing with me, God!" I launched my Bible into the closet and went to sleep. I was crushed. Mistakenly, I went looking for God's voice inside of myself.

The next day, it just so happened that one of my first classes was on hermeneutics, which is the art and science of biblical interpretation. I can't explain how elated I was about this course. **Like**

a soldier training for battle, I was ready. I'll never forget my professor, Dr. Allen, an elderly gentleman who was the jolliest person on campus. Though he was up in age, you couldn't help but see the young professor in him, still just as excited about Jesus and teaching theology as ever. The timing could not have been more perfect. God heard my prayers. I so urgently wanted the necessary tools to study the Bible for myself and not have to solely depend on the opinions and input of others.

NEW VOICES

I wish I could end the story here and say that after taking the hermeneutics class, I lived happily ever after. I was certainly learning a lot and finding much joy in the material and the skills I was developing. However, the more I learned, the more I was confronted by how much I didn't know. Not only that, but I now had much more to wrestle with in terms of knowing where I stood with Christianity in addition to wanting to find a church home.

I confess I was becoming drained trying to manage the schoolwork load after taking nearly four years off from high school, in addition to my theological crisis. My emotional stamina was waning fast. *Does this stuff even matter?* I began to question. I started spending more time being social and less time focusing on my schoolwork. Pondering my theology, wondering who was really saved and who was not, and trying to learn Calvinism was chipping away at my faith. I started to want out. I was ready to quit.

The university required chapel attendance for each student. Typically, I would go hoping for some word of encouragement. Maybe I would hear or see something that would shed light into my darkened and troubled soul. As I entered the chapel one day, I sat near the back. I slumped in my seat and was mostly disengaged. The dean approached the podium and explained that we had a guest speaker that day. As he introduced the speaker, I was fairly neutral in my interest. But I was open to hearing him out.

As the guest preacher took the stage, he had a rather ominous temperament about him. He didn't start off with a cool icebreaker to win the students over or a joke to warm up the crowd. He was very serious. There was something about it that I respected and was drawn to. He started off by saying that many people think they are Christians but really are not. Out came a list of sins and vices he spouted off that he knew took place on a college campus.

"I don't care that this is a Christian campus," he blurted. "Many of you say you love God, but how can you love Him when you're blatantly sinning in His face? When you're in secret sin and pretend to be a child of God? Jesus says, 'If you love Me, keep My commandments,'" he exclaimed.

He continued, "Dare I say, you're not a Christian if you don't have the affections of God. You need to repent and turn to Jesus. You may think that you've been a Christian all these years, but you have never been regenerated and actually converted if your lifestyle hasn't changed."

It was a rather frightening sermon. I began to question my own salvation. *Maybe that's why I've been so down in the dumps lately. Perhaps I'm not even a Christian*, I concluded.

Any assurance of salvation I may have maintained was utterly obliterated. The Law was laid on thick, and I was indeed crushed by it. After his message, I stayed in the chapel and wept profusely. I begged God to save me from my sin. I asked Him for forgiveness for all of my wrongs and to not send me to hell. "Please!" I begged. I was both horrified and hopeful—horrified in that I thought I was a Christian but had too quickly called it into question. Hopeful that God would save me if I called out to Him. It was a curious experience. Oddly enough, it did give a boost to my attitude and mood. While exiting the auditorium, I saw the guest preacher in the parking lot. I got his attention and thanked him for his message and shared my experience.

He gave me a few more layers of Law with a smile, and eventually, we celebrated the Gospel message for sinners. He also suggested that I read the Puritans and learn how to kill my sin and align my affections with the Lord's. "This is pivotal to what it means to be a believer," he insisted. Looking back on the experience, I can see how God used it and worked it out for my good, but I certainly take issue with his preaching approach. Nonetheless, it gave me the spark I needed to continue on my quest for theological stability. I was determined to press onward.

After class one day, a fellow student approached me and asked had I heard of John Piper.

"No, I haven't," I said.

"You have to check him out!" she replied.

She recommended a few books of his and told me he was a Calvinist. One of the books was about one's desires and how we ought to always be seeking to have joy on the inside for God. I thought to myself, *This is perfect. This sounds like the affections spiel from the guy who spoke during chapel. Are these coincidences? I think not.* I had just learned about Calvinism on tour, and it was seeming like Calvinism was the right way to go. The social influence was piling up.

During the same week, another person asked me what church I belonged to.

"I'm actually not a member anywhere at the moment. Long story," I replied.

She suggested that I check out her father's church.

"Who is your pops?" I asked.

She proudly responded, "Dr. McClain."

"Oh, Dr. McClain is your dad? That's pretty cool! I love Dr. McClain," I boasted. He happened to be one of my professors. She told me the name of the church and what times they held service. Finally, a Calvinist church recommendation. I couldn't wait until Sunday.

As Sunday rolled around, I made my way to the church that was recommended. It was an hour drive from my home in the inner city. Good thing I was living on campus at the time! It was only a twenty-five-minute drive from there. Although I was only one of two Black persons in the entire building, I didn't mind at all. **I wanted Jesus, and I wanted sound doctrine.** I sat in on a Sunday morning class taught by my professor. He recognized me and greeted me with a friendly welcome. I felt at home. I thoroughly enjoyed the class. We actually walked verse by verse through Scripture. It was exhilarating! This is what I longed for: a church home that valued theology of the brand that I fell in love with on tour.

I found the pastor to be a kind and genuine person. He saw me and sought me out. I shared a small piece of my story and how I found out about their church home. I was surprised when he extended an invitation to talk more after service. "I'd love that," I stated. I began to visit the church regularly. Conveniently placed in the foyer was a table with books for sale. From it, I was given a stack of books for free. The pastor hand-selected the ones he thought would be good for me as one newly joining the Calvinist brand of Christianity.

I was not expecting that at all. There had to have been at least seven books I took home that day, all expanding on the Calvinist way of processing Christianity. I could not wait to dive in.

"If you have any questions we can go out for coffee and discuss," he offered.

This was a dream. To be able to work through these things with the pastor? I was grateful to God for linking me with a faithful man who took interest in my spiritual journey, a thing for which I am still grateful.

I began to devour the books immediately. Taking notes. Highlighting paragraphs. Underlining potent points. Jotting down questions I wanted to ask the pastor. In addition, I started to research all the authors. I found my favorites and ordered sermons from them online. I obsessed over listening to sermon series while working on campus as a janitor. **It felt like a foretaste of heaven.** Oftentimes, I'd forget I was actually at work. (At least, until I had to clean up an unusually large mess made by rowdy college students.) R. C. Sproul quickly became one of my favorites. He talked a lot about this guy named Martin Luther. He shared his deep love for the Reformation and Luther's contribution to Christianity.

This paired well with the reading from one of the classes on *The Bondage of the Will* by Martin Luther. Luther's name kept coming up. First by my youth pastor as a teen. Next by Cross Movement on the tour. Then in the readings from the free books the pastor gave me, in class, and finally, by one of my new favorite teachers. I was really being drawn to Luther. Yet I didn't make too much of it because he was still being positioned as second chair to John Calvin. The more I read and dove into sermons by Sproul and listened to sermons at the church I was visiting, I was falling deeper and deeper in love with what Calvinists call the doctrines of grace—in particular, the doctrine of God's sovereignty.

PART III

LOOKING
INSIDE MYSELF

CHAPTER 5

LOOKING THROUGH
A CALVINIST LENS

This is where things got interesting. Considering the context of my personal life, one will see how this emphasis on God being in complete control functioned as a healing balm to the complexities of my specific experience. As mentioned, I grew up in the inner city of north St. Louis with two parents who had their own challenges. This primed me for the core emphasis of Calvinism, God's sovereignty. Already, as an African American male, I faced many unique challenges to basic survival and thriving.

Though no country is perfect, being born in brown skin in the United States placed me in an already existing saga with intricate dynamics to figure out. Those challenges were compounded by being raised by my mother, an amazing woman of deep faith but who was diagnosed with schizophrenia and clinical depression, and by my committed and hardworking father, who was for a long time addicted to drugs and alcohol before Jesus gripped his heart and brought him to saving faith. This made the inspirational style of preaching from my "Black church" experience that much more appealing in comparison to what was ahead from the Calvinistic camp.

In my former church context, there was a heavy emphasis

on the simplicity of God's Word and the practicality of living it out. There was a cultural sensitivity to both the systemic and ethnic struggles of the Black experience, packaged in the presentation of Christianity. This included God's love for us, His desire to see us flourish, how we were created in His image and reflect attributes of His own. It reminded us that Jesus thought us worthy to die for and that we were His good creation. Finally, it ended in a commission to spread this Good News to all those like us. This "positive preaching" spoke life into areas that were relevant to the people of our culture.

In contrast, as I began to further embrace Calvinism (from the Reformed Baptist sect), I found a heavy emphasis on the sinfulness of the human race. The doctrine of total depravity informed us how vile we are as humans, undeserving of any good thing. The Puritans were particularly skilled in describing the wretchedness of human beings and elevating God's wrath as His chief attribute. (At times, it felt like His only attribute.) The shift in tone and emphasis was tricky for me, an only child raised in a turbulent home. Particularly challenging was the twisting and bending of my mind to "feel bad" about myself. I already struggled with many doubts, fears, and insecurities about myself, and now I was being coached into thinking even worse things about my personhood.

This apparent dark perspective on who I was before God was difficult to decipher when contrasted with what I was accustomed to hearing from my former church culture. Nevertheless, the emphasis on God's sovereignty caused me to find God behind all deeds, both good and bad. Initially, the Reformed version of sovereignty brought much comfort. It served as an overarching explanation for all the things I struggled to understand about myself, my culture, and my society. Now I knew God was in control and used all the good, bad, and confusing things in my life to happen for my benefit. It made sense at the time.

GOD'S SOVEREIGNTY

Most important, God's sovereignty over who goes to heaven or hell was based on His predestination and good pleasure, Calvinists argued. He secured the place of a select group of chosen ones by sending His Son to die only for them—not for the entire world without exception. In fact, He also decided in advance those He elected (dare I say, created?) for hell.

Welcoming this doctrine into my mind carved an irreparable category in my conscience. In seeps violent terror into my soul. Maybe I would prove to be one of the ones who was never chosen. Or worse, maybe I'm one of the ones God created for hell "or passed over" solely to glorify His wrath. This was a horrid idea I was being disciplined to embrace if I wanted to be faithful to Scripture.

My only hope was to really, really, *really* believe what Jesus accomplished on the cross for my sin and to align my affections and morality up with my profession of faith. This plays out practically by performing more spiritual exploits for God. If one was a musician, it was thought that the person should stop doing "secular" music and start doing Christian music for the Lord. Or if one had interest in a "worldly" endeavor such as sports, then the athlete should abandon that ambition and pursue the overseas mission field. After all, that would be a more "holy" and "spiritual" thing to do and would show God how serious a person is about Him.

This hyperattention to God's sovereignty eventually became morbid and draining. Across many pulpits flowed the preoccupation with explaining what God was up to or thinking on matters that often extended beyond scriptural revelation. For example, many pastors were comfortable giving guesses for why someone had experienced a sudden disease. One might say, "In God's sovereignty, He has caused you to fall ill to glorify Him and to perhaps save you from sinning further. Now that you are bedridden, you no longer have the ability to hang out where you used to go."

It was as if we Reformed folk had God figured out. It started to make Him appear small and more like one of us: less loving and more wrathful. Though God is sovereign and one can draw great comfort from that reality, one can also weaponize it and do great harm to the conscience. So it is with God's wrath. Yes, God has wrath, but it should not be paraded like it's what excites God the most. Nor should we as Christians be excited to highlight it. Luther called God's wrath His foreign attribute, meaning it's the thing He preferred not to draw on. I believe, judging from Scripture (such as Isaiah 28:21), Luther is correct.

PREDESTINATION

This magnified preoccupation with God's wrath is mostly drawn from the Calvinist emphasis of Romans 9. I remember when I first heard the Calvinist explanation of chapter 9 from the Book of Romans. I was petrified! As an average churchgoer from the hood, my Full Gospel Baptist church had never addressed this text. Or perhaps it was addressed minus the added fright and had simply escaped me.

One day at a Bible study led by one of my professors, he explained to us that he'd be teaching on election and predestination. By this point, I was a member of the Reformed Baptist Calvinist church I started off visiting. **I was excited and a bit scared, if I'm honest.** We isolated the chapter and dealt with it as if Paul's intention with Romans 9 was to teach the doctrine of predestination and double predestination. Predestination teaches that God calls people to faith, giving faith to people despite the lack of their worth. Double predestination is the idea that God both elects some for heaven and some for hell.

To put it bluntly, that was wrong and not Paul's intention. Romans 9 should be considered in light of the entire book and, in particular, chapters 8, 10, and 11. Paul is building the case that we are justified by faith and not works. Salvation does not come through bloodline or merit but by faith. Paul draws on a few Old Testament figures to make his point: Abraham, Isaac, Rebekah, Jacob, Esau, and Pharaoh, to name a few. He uses these people to show that there is Old Testament precedent for his line of reasoning, that God chooses not on the basis of works or lineage but by grace. I wish my professor would have rightly taught us Romans 9:13:

As it is written, "Jacob I loved, but Esau I hated."

This verse is not about their eternal state or individual salvation (besides, later, the two bros reconciled). But this was about God's free choice to choose Jacob to be the carrier of the people of Israel, through whom the Messiah came. This is in contrast to Esau, who was the porter of Edom, a wicked nation. Paul assumes people would contend for some injustice in God. "That's not fair!"

they might say. So here is Romans 9:14–15:

> What shall we say then? Is there injustice on God's
> part? By no means! For He says to Moses, "I will
> have mercy on whom I have mercy, and I will have
> compassion on whom I have compassion."

The context is this: why has God left Israel in their hardened state? Like God did with Pharaoh, He allowed Israel and Pharaoh to persist in their already existing rebellion. It was an act of judgment and not a random, unconditional decision. He turned them over to what they genuinely wanted: to do their own thing. God hardens after the persons have given themselves over to wickedness.

I wish my professor would have rightly taught us Romans 9:22–23:

> What if God, desiring to show His wrath and to
> make known His power, has endured with much
> patience vessels of wrath prepared for destruction,
> in order to make known the riches of His glory for
> vessels of mercy, which He has prepared before-
> hand for glory?

It was not teaching double predestination (that God made some for hell). Keep in mind that hell was created for the devil and his angels, not for people.

Matthew 25:41:

> Then He will say to those on His left, "Depart from
> Me, you cursed, into the eternal fire prepared for
> the devil and his angels."

A more careful reading of Romans 9:22–23 exposes what the text says. God has "endured with much patience." The text does *not* say God prepared vessels, people, for wrath. Paul only asks:

what if God endured these vessels to show His power and wrath to make known His mercy and glory? **The whole of Scripture credits the sinner and the devil for sinful rebellion.** Therefore, it is safe to conclude that human beings who insist on resisting God's gracious call to repentance and faith are responsible for their own hardening.

The passage *does* say, explicitly and clearly, that God has prepared vessels (people) of mercy beforehand for glory! Romans 9:23:

> In order to make known the riches of His glory for vessels of mercy, which He has prepared before-hand for glory.

When it comes to God's ordaining, He is actively doing one and is not actively doing the other. He is calling people to faith, but He is not condemning others to unbelief.

Again, the context is salvation by faith, not works. Why do some Gentiles believe and some children of Abraham do not believe? It has to do with faith, a gift from God, and not bloodline.

Having said all that, Paul still has hope!

Romans 11:32:

> For God has consigned all to disobedience, that He may have mercy on all.

Yes, it's true. There is universal condemnation under the Law, and yet, Paul notes, it ends with universal grace. All those who believe by faith will benefit.

God's love, patience, and grace-giving heart should be noticed by His long-suffering with sinful humanity. What a powerful image of forbearance these verses illustrate. Such piercing truth. Such sobering revelation. God is kind and gracious to all.

Continuing on, Romans 10:21:

> All day long I have held out My hands to a disobedient and contrary people.

God is *wanting* His people to come home.

Paul is *aching* for his kinsman to find rest.

Romans 9:3:

> For I could wish that I myself were accursed and cut off from Christ for the sake of my brothers, my kinsmen according to the flesh.

Yet, unfortunately, in the face of their Savior's outstretched arms, Matthew 23:37:

> O Jerusalem, Jerusalem, the city that kills the prophets and stones those who are sent to it! How often would I have gathered your children together as a hen gathers her brood under her wings, and you were not willing!

Therefore, God gave Israel over to what they wanted. Their own way.

This does not sound like a God who created people solely for hell to glorify His wrath.

This does not sound like an apostle who believes His God handcrafted a large portion of humans to suffer in eternal hellfire because it brings Him glory. **This sounds like a God who endured with patience (Romans 9:22).**

One may say, "But wait, Romans 9:20–21 clearly demonstrates

that God created both vessels: one for eternal punishment and the other for mercy eternal, beforehand."

> While it is said of the vessels of mercy in the active voice that God had afore prepared them unto glory, the passive voice is used of the vessels of wrath: ready, ripe for destruction. The passive construction is not to be regarded as accidental, but as intended, since the vessels of wrath and the vessels of mercy are here compared. The more we note how the words "Which He had afore prepared unto glory" emphasizes God's work in the vessels of mercy, the more it strikes us that in regard to the vessels of wrath, in so far as they are "fitted to destruction," there is no mention whatever of any "doing" by God. The preparation for glory and the fitting unto damnation do not have the same author.[1]

Furthermore, Romans 9:22 does *not* contain the word *beforehand* related to vessels of wrath. However, Romans 9:23 *does* contain the word *beforehand* related to vessels of mercy.

You start to notice this elsewhere as it relates to God preparing a place for vessels of mercy.

Matthew 25:34:

> Then the King will say to those on His right, "Come, you who are blessed by My Father, inherit the kingdom prepared for you from the foundation of the world."

As it relates to God preparing a place for vessels of wrath in Matthew 25:41:

> Then He will say to those on His left, "Depart from

---

1 Francis Pieper, *Christian Dogmatics*, vol. 3 (St. Louis: Concordia Publishing House, 1953), 497.

Me, you cursed, into the eternal fire prepared for
the devil and his angels."

God's kingdom was prepared for people. Hell was prepared
for the devil. See what Paul says about God's desire for people in
1 Timothy 2:4:

[He] desires all people to be saved and to come to
the knowledge of the truth.

People are themselves considered responsible for resisting
God. Selah.

Looking back on Bible class that day, I now think it would have
been helpful if the professor would have at least exposed us to
other ways Romans 9 has been exposited. Particularly those from
the Lutheran Reformation, seeing as we share a similar sentiment
for the first Reformer, Martin Luther. Before I became a Calvinist,
I had little appetite for election and predestination, if any at all.
But for those who join Calvinism, there becomes an unusually
heavy emphasis placed on it. Yes, it's taught in Scripture (a sweet
doctrine meant to comfort), but the Calvinist brand of emphasis
is unique. You move from being election malnourished to a glutton
for it. Next, it becomes the lens through which you view yourself,
others, and the whole of the Scriptures. Am I elect? Is he elect?
Was she ever truly elect or was she never with us in the first place?
Don't worry about who the elect are, just preach the Gospel to all;
the elect will come. Election. Election. Election. And so it goes.
This, in turn, impacts your style of biblical interpretation.

This misinterpretation is the result of isolating verses and
viewing Scripture through a system. It is also the result of not
letting Scripture interpret Scripture, which is a basic principle of

interpretation. The goal is the simple and plain meaning of the text. **When people are more committed to logical consistency within their systematic theology than they are with what Scripture reveals, the result is off-kilter teaching, outright false doctrine, and wounded consciences.** In this case, this sends people to look within to their feelings, to their personal performance, and to their level of sincerity—all hoping to find proof of genuine conversion.

LACK OF CERTAINTY

Eighteen years of being traumatized by certain interpretations haunted my soul. Another weaponized passage was Matthew 7:21–23:

> Not everyone who says to Me, "Lord, Lord," will enter the kingdom of heaven, but the one who does the will of My Father who is in heaven. On that day many will say to Me, "Lord, Lord, did we not prophesy in Your name, and cast out demons in Your name, and do many mighty works in Your name?" And then will I declare to them, "I never knew you; depart from Me, you workers of lawlessness."

This text is often used against the average churchgoer who is struggling with a troubled conscience. Ignored in many cases is the context of this section, which is confronting false prophets—those who are purposefully being deceptive for personal gain. However, the emphasis that often makes it across the pulpits, into popular books, and within podcasts is that it is possible to think you are a Christian but to actually, on the Day of Judgment, discover you have never been known by Jesus.

This is frightening because many hear it as saying that you can be a faithful believer—actively serving in ministry or church work or simply living an innocent, pious life—and for some unknown reason, you will one day hear Jesus say, "Depart from Me, you worker of iniquity, for I never knew you." This is a nuclear missile to the troubled conscience, a terrible misuse of the Law for those who are contrite over their sin and are desperately in need of absolution and assurance.

To overcome such fears, people feel that they must thrust themselves on the mercies of their conversion experience and their progression in spiritual growth (often spoken of as sanctification). Did you really change and go from darkness to light? Are you hating your sin more and more each day? Are you checking your heart's motivations for your good deeds? Are you glorifying God in increasing measures as you expand your satisfaction in Him? And so on. But this does not lead to comfort, just more internal searching.

Is every day miserable for those in the Reformed camp? Not at all. Actually, I'd say most days people live in the assurance of faith alone. Praise God for that! However, when those dark clouds come looming, the storm that strikes is usually unbearable. It is frightening enough to snatch the strongest person's faith in an instant. And unfortunately, I've witnessed just that from many.

CHAPTER 6

LIVING CALVINIST

In 2004, I released my first solo album to the masses. I had released other projects locally, but now that I was signed to a major independent label, I was sure to reach more people. By that point, I was fully persuaded that Calvinism was the true exposition of the Scriptures. I was overwhelmingly convinced that the five-point TULIP was biblical. What is the five-point TULIP, you ask? It's an acronym used to get at the gist of Calvinism, though Calvin himself did not codify it. The *T* stands for *total depravity*. The *U* stands for *unconditional election*. The *L* stands for *limited atonement*. The *I* stands for *irresistible grace*. The *P* stands for *perseverance of the saints*.

Total depravity describes humanity's fallen condition due to Adam's sin. The basic idea is that human beings are completely sinful, corrupt, and fallen beyond repair. It states that we are born dead in sin and can do nothing on our own to bring spiritual life to ourselves. It is not saying that humans are as bad as they can be but that every area of our humanity is sinfully broken: our intellect, imagination, thoughts, and deeds, to name a few. Lutherans are okay with this idea but would prefer the language of Luther himself: the "bondage of the will," meaning that the will is bound by sin and cannot choose God. We'd prefer to avoid misconceptions and misunderstandings that can be derived from the language of total depravity.

Unconditional election describes the idea that God does not choose to elect a person on the basis of some "good" He sees in them, some potential, and thus wants to recruit them to His team. Nor does God look down the corridors of time to see who would eventually choose Him and then chooses them on that basis. Unconditional election argues that God decides to elect a person for His own holy reasons. Here, Lutherans can "amen" this understanding. It is consistent with Scripture and with what Luther handed down.

Limited atonement is the notion that Jesus only died for a limited number of people—that He did not die for all people without exception. Calvinists would say Jesus went to the cross to die only for the elect. Continuing, they'd add that His atonement is powerful enough and not lacking in stretch to cover everyone's sin but that His intention was simply not to die for the sins of every human being. This is the false notion we've addressed several times already.

Irresistible grace is the idea that once a person receives the inward call of Jesus (as opposed to the outward general call that goes to everyone) they cannot resist. They will want to come to faith in Christ and will therefore not resist, because they cannot resist. It's argued that the inward call brings with it new life—new eyes to see how good God is—and so a person will want to be a Christian. Some call it regeneration, which is new life given to the person by the Holy Spirit. This idea sounds great, but unfortunately, the Bible argues otherwise in many places. It appears that many resist God and that in God's freedom, He has chosen to make Himself resistible. Why? The Bible doesn't explain that nor does it give us permission to start guessing.

Perseverance of the saints teaches that God will preserve His saints unto the end, that no true Christian can lose salvation. This teaching struggles to handle the biblical reality that, unfortunately, apostasy is a real category. In other words, true Christians in the Bible and in our contemporary experience actually decide to walk away from their faith and thus lose the benefits of what Jesus earned for them on the cross. Lutherans, along with Scripture, would rightly argue that a person who walked away from faith can repent and receive again the benefits of salvation. We'd say, "Return to your Baptism." More on that later.

Album after album, I gave myself to creatively expositing TULIP in art form. **I introduced for the first time many popular Reformed Baptist pastors and influencers to the Christian rap community.** This isn't to say others did not know about them, but I was vocal about publicly sharing the preachers I was drawing knowledge from. This led to many collaborations, conferences, concerts, and other outreach efforts. Most of my closest friends by this point had also become Calvinist thinkers. Eventually, I met other artists and laypersons alike from across the United States who were also being impacted by this budding momentum surrounding Calvinistic thought.

WE WERE DRAWN BY THE TEACHING ASPECT

The game changer for most of us was the emphasis on the Bible. Calvinism, in a great way, brought with it a prioritization of knowing your Bible. Also important was the notion of elevating Scripture above all else, above your feelings and experiences. We were discontent with much of the theatrics that came along with church life in many of our communities.

For many of us, while we were gaining a great deal of helpful foundational tools and teaching from the Charismatic Church, there wasn't as much of an emphasis on theology and doctrine. Calvinism was keen on answering questions, knowing the truth, and being sound. This was attractive to us young millennials. We wanted answers. **We wanted to use our minds and not just our hearts.**

We simply weren't the type of people who were okay going to church wearing suits and asking no questions. We were curious and bold enough to be different from our parents' generation. We asked questions such as, "Where in the Bible does it say Jesus is God? How do we know God wants us to be rich and to not get sick? What's wrong with listening to rap music? Why does God care whether we wear shorts, a hat, and flip-flops to church? What does this word mean in the original language?"

Calvinism provided a space for us to ask these types of questions of the Scriptures. We were all being taught that the Bible has a lot to say about these matters and that Church history should also be considered. We felt like kids with an unlimited budget in the app store! Finally, a Christian space that welcomed our youthful curiosity and gave us a platform to be heard.

However, the catch was we that had to stop teaching that Jesus died for everyone. We had to start teaching that if Jesus died for everyone, and some of the people He died for ended up in hell, then that would mean some of Jesus' blood was wasted. These emphases brought about social strain with many of our families, church homes, and friendships. And for those of us who were recording artists, the strain reached into our lyrics—not to mention our public representation of the nature of God. We were forced to describe God as one who is so concerned about His own glory that He would create some just for hell, to glorify His glory.

I recall standing on stage in Kingston, Jamaica. I looked at a crowd of hundreds and hundreds of people and wanted to tell them that Jesus died for them. But I couldn't. I took a deep breath, closed my eyes, and simply spewed off something like, "Jesus loves us and died for all those who would believe." That was it. I felt horrible. I felt like I lied to them. Yet, my Calvinist-informed conscience restricted my verbiage. **I admit, I struggled deeply just to get through that concert.** It was as if the Holy Spirit was grieved and was tugging at my heart that I had been unfaithful to the Gospel. Had I? It was a strange and conflicting experience. Why would the Spirit be disappointed? Aren't I communicating "sound doctrine"? By this point, I was well into my Reformed Baptist journey and had grown accustomed to speaking and thinking that way. Yet out of nowhere, somehow, the Spirit's voice cut through my seemingly impenetrable layers of carefully crafted Calvinistic convictions and quietly whispered 1 Timothy 4:9–10:

> The saying is trustworthy and deserving of full
> acceptance. For to this end we toil and strive,
> because we have our hope set on the living God,
> who is the Savior of all people, especially of those
> who believe.

Sometimes, I reimagine myself on that same stage, in that same moment, but this time, with my eyes open and a heart full of scriptural theology that Jesus *is* the Savior of the world! He is the Savior of *all* people. The question becomes this: Are you going to, by faith, subjectively receive what has already been objectively purchased for you? Or will you resist what is yours: salvation, Christ? This time, I would make the same distinction Paul made: "the living God, who is the Savior of all people, especially of those who believe."

If we are not listening carefully, we wrongly hear this as teaching universalism (that everyone will go to heaven). That is not the case at all. Neither Paul nor his audience assumed universalism follows from this train of thought. The text states plainly that Christ is the Savior of all but uniquely of those who believe. Yes, Jesus is the Savior of the world, but only by faith alone does one receive the benefits of salvation. However, it would be a while before I would come to realize this. I still had more time to run down on the Calvinistic clock before it would end its era in my life.

Though a lot of what I was taught for eighteen years wasn't the most faithful to the Bible, God did a host of great things through it. He's always taking our two fish and five loaves and multiplying them to feed the masses. I'd say it felt like what many have called a revival. All across the world, from the late '90s but really gaining steam around 2004, people from the inner city were hearing of the Gospel of Jesus Christ filtered through Calvinism and gaining interest in Bible college or theological education in some fashion. Conferences were starting. Church planting started to become a hot topic. God was saving and sending many. You could count on everyone having a Wayne Grudem systematic theology book and a John MacArthur study Bible. These tools functioned as GPSes through the paths of Scripture. We were all drinking from the same fountains.

TIME FOR SPECULATION

Another thing to note is that we were all in the same place in life, either teenagers or young adults fresh out of high school. Most people were single or in the endless loony cycle of dating and trying to figure out, based on God's sovereignty, if He knew who your spouse was going to be in advance, whom you were predestined to marry, or if we have the free will to choose. Or maybe it was both. Off we went with the freedom to speculate. Without wives or husbands, children, or mortgages, most people had a lot of space to ponder. We had the budget to blow money on a bunch of book purchases and sermon series on CD. **Plus, we had the time to spend countless hours hanging out and talking (or fellowshiping, to use a "holier" word).**

The conversations were sparkling! They were riveting with deep theological waxing. Topics included what God was doing in eternity past. Would we rejoice with God over loved ones who did not make it to heaven? If we got to heaven and God was not there, would we want to still be there or not? We considered how easy it is to make an idol out of anything. I confess, it was fun to explore the unknown, to go beyond the revelation of Scripture, and to make guesses as to what God may or may not have been up to. Yes, we had an expanded appetite for speculation. That was common practice and was not healthy, biblically.

Our minds were heavily conditioned to wonder and to go beyond the written Word of God. We mostly couched this in the verbiage of "God's sovereignty," as understood by the Reformed and in keeping with Calvin himself, who often felt the need to close many of the gaps left open in Scripture (such as his teaching on double predestination, as mentioned earlier). I've heard it described this way: if there was a circle left open right where it might close, Martin Luther was okay leaving it open, but John Calvin felt the need to close it. I think that is a fair statement.

I remember listening to a sermon series and hearing a statement that made my jaw drop and my heart sink to my toes. When asked about deceased loved ones who did not turn to the Lord, a popular Calvinist pastor said that in heaven, we will be so in touch with God's glory, and will have so much in common with Jesus, that we will rejoice and celebrate that our loved ones who did not repent are in hell. He was careful to add that it would certainly be unhealthy to rejoice in that way now. Besides, he said, during this dispensation of time, we have more in common with one another and cannot imagine such a thing. But in heaven, we will finally have more in common with God and will feel what He feels, and thus, we will be able to rejoice that God is being glorified in His wrath, expressed in eternal punishment.

My stomach turned upon hearing this. Yet I desired to feel what God felt. I wanted to align with His affections. Furthermore, if one was troubled by this notion, the pastor offered this comfort: he instructed us to accept this reality but also to not like it—that was the healthiest way forward, he exclaimed.

Again, this type of speculation was normal. Here are a few more examples:

- Why are some saved and not others? Because God elected some for heaven and created others for hell. Double predestination.

- Since the road to hell is wide and the path to heaven is narrow, more people will be in hell than in heaven.

- Why did God let that young Christian girl die so young? Because He did not want her to continue sinning and lose more heavenly rewards.

- Crazy to see that guy walk away from his faith. He was such a strong believer. What happened? He did not walk away; he was never with us in the first place. Even though he appeared and professed faith for decades, he was deceived and deceived man.

These indeed are devilish ponderings!

The writings of Martin Luther, the first reformer, among others, contribute a needed perspective related to these matters. There are many who need nursing back to theological and spiritual health so that they can reimagine God rightly after having heavily overdosed on mounds of unhealthy speculative doctrines.

The Bible teaches us to rest in our limitations and trust. Deuteronomy 29:29:

> The secret things belong to the LORD our God, but the things that are revealed belong to us and to our children forever.

Lord, in Your kindness, please liberate many. In Your Son's name we pray. Amen.

WORKING THROUGH THEOLOGY

Under the influence of "the new Calvinism," developing our theology during this pivotal point in the life cycle as we all began to age, we cemented our livelihood around our theology. Many teens from across the US and beyond became adult pastors. Many earned bachelor's, master's, or even doctoral degrees from Calvinist institutions. A host of people became college professors. Others grew to be popular recording artists. Some morphed into YouTube personalities. A great deal became social media influencers and podcasters. Some were blessed to become mothers who trained their children to think about salvation and the Sacraments like a Reformed person would.

Over time, your theology influences how you make money, how you interact with friends and family, how you engage new people, and how you view the world around you. It impacts how you see the past, how you interpret the present, and how you imagine the future. Your theology gets everywhere, sort of how sand does when you spend an entire day at the beach. You find sand in all manner of invading places.

Day after day, year after year, you constantly reinforce your worldview through regular church attendance, prayer requests, Bible studies, Christian conversation, and personal application. Over the course of time, you are so convinced you are correct in your thinking that you can't imagine how people who do not think like you can even survive. You almost pity them, at worst.

At best, you earnestly beg God to bring them to "the light" and to see and understand the Bible, theology, and the world exactly like you and your camp.

Even if someone presents a healthy challenge to your doctrinal stance, you have a well-developed muscle for mental gymnastics. You can twist and turn in all manner of contorted forms to maintain consistency with your particular way of interpreting Scripture. In fact, you have tailor-cut arguments and answers crafted to ward off the opponent's theology. Your timeline is a well-documented archive that displays the full range of your defense of Calvinism. Your text message thread is a personal manuscript of your engagement on an array of subjects through your theological filters and framework. Your humor. Your anger. Your advice. All rooted in the TULIP. What is life even, outside of your echo chamber?

CUTTING THROUGH THE WALLS

What can possibly cut through your intellectual defensive wall? Your immense level of comfort and familiarity? Under what circumstance would you even be able to position yourself to ask age-old questions about the doctrinal stance you developed decades ago? You've heard all the arguments against your theological position many moons ago. You swat those down as easily as a fly attempting to land on your nose. What possible set of events would even remotely cause you to reexamine your paradigm?

I'm not typically a heavy sleeper. I can hear the slightest noise and wake up. Nor do I have a lot of dreams. I used to dream a lot as a kid. Well, they were mostly nightmares. Every day that I'd wake up from a bad dream, I'd beg God to stop me from having dreams altogether. Eventually, it seems He answered my prayer because I stopped having dreams for years. Or I simply had no recollection of them once I woke up.

Yet sometimes, when I hit that REM sleep, I'm done. Nothing can wake me. Not an uncomfortable position destined to leave a crick in my neck, nothing. However, the most interesting thing happens when I feel the urge to use the restroom while in a deep sleep. Pardon me for dragging you this close into my personal life, but here we go.

This is brilliant to me. God, You are an amazing genius! Since my members can't talk, how do they signal to me to wake up when I'm in REM sleep? Every time, without question, my brain will develop a frightening plot that communicates fear to my emotions. That somehow affects my mood while I'm sleeping and signals to my brain uncomfortably. That strong sense of discomfort will kick me out of REM sleep and wake up my physical sensory. I'm then made aware that I have to use the restroom, and off we go! Wow! God designed my body (I don't know how it works for you) to communicate with me under seemingly impossible circumstances by using discomfort, fear, and something bad. Just wow!

That may not be mind-blowing to you, but to me, it's incredible! God made a way for my body to talk to me, even talking me out of REM sleep. Insert mind-blown emoji here! It's a pattern I can count on every single time. What's my point? Often, when it seems that we are deathly gripped in a mindset that has us completely gridlocked, it takes something bad or scary to shake us awake. I see this pattern over and over when I watch documentaries on people who have escaped a cult or a relationship with a manipulative person.

There's the stage where you are 100 percent convinced that everything is just fine. You can't imagine life any other way. Even if someone you love and trust comes to you and says, "Hey, you know I love you. I'm genuinely concerned for you. I think this group you are with is a cult." Or, "This guy/girl you are with is manipulating you." You would not believe the person. Even with mounds of evidence and impenetrable proof, you have developed your mental muscle to perform all the necessary mental gymnastics to see things your way, resulting in the clear-minded person being wrong and you being right.

The only consistent thing I've seen to work for those caught in a cult or trapped in a manipulative relationship is for them to finally see or experience something themselves that so badly frightens them, they are shaken awake from their REM sleep.

From there, things often fall into place quickly. They start to notice everything. Things begin to make sense. Events or experiences they may have noticed but ignored begin to rise to the surface. Past moments emerge to the forefront that they may have tucked away for survival. They begin to connect dots. All the reinterpretation of weird and inconsistent things they dismissed almost immediately become apparent, and the person, in a panic, wants out!

By no means am I calling Calvinism a cult or a manipulative relationship. Please do not hear me saying that. **What I am saying is that when you are so heavily steeped in any school of thought and have built your life around it, it may take an intense experience to help break you out, to open you up to engage a different or potentially better thing.** I found this to be true for many that I know who have left the Calvinist construct of Christianity.

Over time, I, too, started to question things I had embraced theologically. There is a popular mantra used by a well-known Reformed Baptist pastor, beloved by many: "God is most glorified in us when we are most satisfied in Him." This statement used to bring me life! Oh, how I wanted to glorify God. Oh, how I, more than anything, wanted to be satisfied in Him alone, in greater and more radical degrees. Yet that qualifying adverb *most* functioned like a bully. It stood fixed with a mean face and refused to budge, like the Law. "Most glorified." That word kept me striving and chasing but never grasping. It was a moving target. No matter how much I prayed, shared my faith, read my Bible, monitored my motives, nurtured genuine and pure affections "for God," resisted temptation, and attended church service, that one word said, "Not enough! Most!" Needless to say, I spiritually collapsed under the heavy weight of the Law. I could not keep up with the demanding pace of *most*. I realized this statement masquerades as a "Gospel imperative" but underneath is really the mean face of the Law. I realized it never had plans on giving me finality. It only demands more and more. "Most!" it yells. That's all it can do. Little did I know, I would soon be rightly oriented and would no longer have the Gospel mingled with the Law and the Law mingled with the Gospel. This would come by learning the Lutheran emphasis on the proper distinction between Law and Gospel.

Soon, I would learn that I satisfy God because I am in Christ, not based on the qualifying word and expectation *most*. It is Christ whom God the Father is satisfied with, ultimately, and I am hidden in Him. Therefore, God is pleased with me. Soon, I would hear that I glorify God by serving my neighbor based on Matthew 25:34–40. Performing good deeds for the sake of those around me—that makes God smile and the people happy.

And even when I am not most satisfied in Him, I glorify God. How, you ask? My dissatisfaction was absorbed on the cross. **As I continue to trust in my God by faith, I am pleasing to the Father, for Christ's sake.** This because all my good deeds are considered good only because I am hidden in Christ. Otherwise, the Bible says that my righteousness is that of a filthy rag (see Isaiah 64:6). There's no good in me that meets God's perfect standard or that impresses Him, neither before one is a Christian nor after Baptism or conversion. We are seen as right with God by Christ alone.

QUITTING CHRISTIANITY?

One day after a Sunday church gathering, I broke on the inside. I remember the sermon was about more. More affections. More right desires. More internal examination. I came home and sat on the staircase in my living room and simply hung my head low. "I can't do this anymore," I whispered to myself. I was tired. I felt like I simply wasn't doing enough killing the flesh, enough hating my sin, or enough despising the world. I was trying and trying. Working and working. Putting myself in position to do more. Yet that sermon that Sunday was the death blow.

I remember thinking to myself and lightweight praying to God, saying, "Lord, I don't know if I can be a Christian anymore. I just can't give You what You want." As a trained Reformed Baptist

Calvinist with one degree in theology at the time, I knew the right answers and could have corrected my thinking in a self-led theological dialogue. That wasn't the problem. I'm talking spiritually and emotionally, on a personal and pragmatic level. I was tired and ready to tap out.

The thoughts that ran through my mind went like this: *I know Arminianism isn't the right way. I can't go to any church or denomination influenced by them. After all, the TULIP acronym was developed by the theological war between them and the Calvinists.* As a Reformed Baptist Calvinist, I was trained to think the worst about Roman Catholics, so I didn't even consider becoming Roman. The Eastern Church wasn't even mentioned in the Reformed Baptist space. What other alternatives were there? Christianity, it seemed, was reduced to only two options: Calvinism or Arminianism. It felt impossible to simply stop believing that God exists. **For that reason, I deeply considered living as a spiritual nomad.**

The expectation to perform at an Ivy League–level sanctification was all too commonplace. One day as I sat listening to a popular Reformed Baptist pastor, he spoke of sanctification in terms of a letter grade. He exclaimed that some may have a C in sanctification while others may have a B-. My mind drifted as I began to contemplate what grade I might have. I thought to myself, *Well, based on a few nights ago, maybe a D+. But based on the last few days, I'd say at least a C+.* Because I was hypertrained and hyperfocused on monitoring my motives and affections, I was careful to not pridefully grade myself too high on the scale. After all, God was watching and knows my heart. From there, I simply spiraled downward into a brief pit of despair.

During my time in that space, I'd argue that sanctification was arranged in the room in such a way that one constantly would stub their toe. While there were excellent affirmations of forgiveness arranged in the room, the blurred lines between Law and Gospel hindered the smooth path and often led me to stumble. Sanctification was awkwardly placed, out of place. With an unhealthy notion of progress or focus on an upward climb on the ladder of spiritual wins, I was left to believe that the Christian life centers on trying harder: growing closer and closer and closer and closer to Jesus. More effort, more self-denial, more Godly affections, more evangelistic/missional activities, and more obedience. For God! Not to mention, I have to have JOY! while exerting such pietistic energy.

While each of those things have their place, they must be arranged in the room properly, or one will become consumed by either despair or pride.

When we swing on the pendulum of pride and despair, there is no certain answer to the question "What does God think of me?" Moment to moment it changes drastically, fearfully.[2]

The result of this Christian paradigm leads to the following:

- Lowering the bar. This makes you feel better about your lifestyle, living in the false comfort that you are not that bad or the false comfort that you are "killing it."

- Hypocrisy. You are smiling and performing what's expected on the outside while dying on the inside.

2   Bryan Wolfmueller, *Has American Christianity Failed?* (St. Louis: Concordia Publishing House, 2016), 24.

- Comparing yourself to others. "At least I'm not as bad as them." "I'm pretty good." Or, "They are killing it." "I suck."

The Christian life should be centered around Jesus and the proclamation of His Good News: the promise of forgiveness, the comfort of the conscience, the assurance of salvation. Our good works (spiritual growth, spiritual disciplines, sanctification, acts of service, whatever you want to call them) are for the benefit of our neighbor as unto the Lord. They do *not* assist you before God, neither before faith nor during your Christian journey. Furthermore, they are the result of repentance (contrition/remorse and faith). That repentance is created in you by God's Word. By the Spirit. By His power. We get *no* credit in repentance. God's Law accuses and condemns us, kills us and drowns us. This leads to contrition. God's Gospel (proclamation of forgiveness) then revives us and brings us up out of the water into new life! By faith, that is to say, trust in Jesus, we receive the forgiveness of our sins.

Indeed, the Christian life is a life of repentance. What does that mean, though? It means that we constantly live in our Baptism. We are constantly being accused by God's good Law. We drown underneath the condemnation of the Law. Then, Christ resuscitates us with the announcement of our forgiveness. **He brings us out of the water and back to life.** This is the Gospel. From there, we "bear fruit in keeping with repentance" (Matthew 3:8). The fruit is the result of repentance. Our neighbor then benefits. This cycle continues until Jesus calls us home.

The Law says "do," the Gospel says "done." The Law commands, the Gospel promises. The Law measures and judges, the Gospel forgives. The Law tells us how we ought to live, the Gospel tells us that Jesus died; and He died with a marvelous and gracious purpose: to save sinners. Both the Law and the Gospel are from God, but they have different purposes. The Law condemns. The Gospel saves.[3]

If one is not clear on these things, it can certainly rob your faith and lead you away from Christianity altogether. That's where I was headed. I gave nearly two decades to the synchronization of my heart's affections with God's affections. I maintained faithful church membership and accountability. I vigorously exercised living in community with transparency. I read all the prominent scholars and lay leaders. I attended all the big conferences. Organically, I met and made friends with many prominent Reformed pastors, leaders, and influencers. I faithfully spread the Reformed doctrines of grace. I attained a bachelor's degree in biblical counseling from the crème de la crème of Reformed Bible institutions so as to attack this deep-seated disconnect between my head and my heart. I was dead set on helping others who struggled like I did, only to find ineffective and insufficient solutions. The theology was disjointed from the reality of the human experience. It took time for me to realize that. As one ages, life moves further and further away from being simple. Things depart from the black and white only, and gray areas start to arise more regularly. The paradoxes and complexities of adulthood don't allow you the luxury of seeing the world as you once had.

PART IV

EXTRA NOS

CHAPTER 7

HUNGRY FOR MORE

Amid this fog, I "randomly" got a phone call from a dear friend of mine who is more like a brother. He was a student in seminary, completing his master's degree.

He told me his Reformed Baptist college professor recommended Concordia Seminary in St. Louis for further training. His boast was that they had a more robust and rigorous academic program. He knew that I, too, was interested in going back to seminary, so he reached out to share the recommendation. Since I trust him, I was excited to pay the school a visit.

Immediately, I contacted the school to inquire about their graduate program. We scheduled a time for me to visit the campus. Once I arrived on campus, I fell in love with the Germanic architecture. I felt like I would enjoy studying there. I didn't quite understand that the school was a Lutheran one. While touring the campus with Rev. Dr. Gerhard H. Bode, I spent some time talking his head off about John Calvin and how much I loved Calvin's contribution to Christianity. Dr. Bode humored me for a time but eventually picked up on the fact that I might have been unaware that the school was confessionally Lutheran. Gracefully, he interjected into the conversation the Lutheran theological tradition that the institution taught. A kind gentleman he is.

Even after finding out it was a Lutheran school, I wrongfully thought Luther and John Calvin were lockstep on all things and pretty much the same guy. I even sat in on a class led by Rev. Dr. Leopoldo A. Sánchez. He was teaching on the doctrine of the Trinity. That was a subject that was dear to me. On a couple of my albums, I dedicated a few songs to the topic and the many theological wars waged both for and against the triune nature of our matchless God. The class was delightful, and Dr. Sánchez was not only brilliant and articulate but also kindhearted and funny. Those characteristics stuck out to me based on the way he conducted the class. We continued the tour, and I got to have lunch with Dr. Bode and Rev. Dr. David R. Maxwell. It was a great day.

I thought to myself, *Sold! I'm in!* The next steps were to enroll and test into the school's graduate program. I received a stack of books in the mail. Time to start studying. Success! I tested into the master's program and was accepted into the school. I was excited!

Wait, did this guy just say Baptism regenerates? Is this book upside down? Yet there was enough familiarity there that kept me interested in reading. I began to notice more blatant nuances that diverged from what I knew of the Reformation. Wait, did the professor just say, "Here's where John Calvin got it wrong?" I was both taken aback and curious. We were discussing the nature of faith and justification in one of my introductory courses, The Lutheran Mind. Rev. Dr. Joel P. Okamoto was the instructor. I was drawn to his genius way of explaining things.

Throughout that quarter, I was confronted with "new" views on universal atonement and the Lord's Supper. The Lord's Supper was particularly interesting to me. I had never heard such an understanding of it. And once again, baptismal regeneration—a very provocative doctrine for the average person influenced by generic American Evangelicalism. As for me, a Reformed Baptist thinker at the time, I was flabbergasted by the notion that God would use His Word coupled with water to deliver His gift of salvation. And to save infants with it too? How dare they assert such things! *Heresy!* my mind screamed.

Yet I was confronted with Scripture, which led me to a fork in the road. **Do I go with what the Scriptures actually say? Or do I distort them to fit my paradigm? I chose not to choose.** My approach was to sit and soak. I listened keenly to every word from each one of my professors' mouths. I profusely took notes, almost transcribing word for word what was said. I even recorded each lecture with the voice memo app on my phone. I would leave campus and play the entire lecture back on my car ride home. I obsessed over what I was learning. Even when I got home, I would decompress from class and then play the voice memos back.

I was being deeply challenged. I was being confronted with concepts and ideas about my Lord, the Bible, and Church history that I simply had not come across during my eighteen years in the Calvinistic space and the entire duration of my exposure to Christianity. At times, it felt a bit overwhelming, but my predominant sentiment was one of curiosity and joy. I was happy to be exposed to so much that I hadn't heard before. I was cautious to comb through everything to make sure I was understanding it correctly, at least from the Lutheran perspective.

I celebrated that I was being educated as opposed to being indoctrinated; unfortunately, what happens in many cases is that students are taught what to believe as opposed to learning how to consider matters broadly and to arrive at the most sound conclusion. I had to grapple with a wide array of Christian thought. Our reading wasn't limited to people who thought exactly as we did. We read much from those outside the Lutheran tradition, even from persons outside the faith. Obviously, everything was in the context of the goal of the institution and being understood from the Christian worldview, the Lutheran paradigm, and ultimately filtered through the lens of holy writ. However, we were still being prepared to use our minds astutely for the sake of Christ and neighbor. It was an amazing time with ever-lingering effects.

DR. JOEL BIERMANN

Soon, I would land in class with a professor by the name of Rev. Dr. Joel D. Biermann. His lectures were uniquely fine-tuned and extremely clear. He pulled no punches either. He was very black and white when he made his point. He certainly was a man of great nuance when it came to considering each facet of a thing. However, after he took you on a journey throughout the gray, he would, with keen precision, direct you back to the black and white of a thing. He's brilliant.

I was drawn to his teaching style. Another important thing about Dr. Biermann was his inclusion of contrast between Lutherans and Calvinists. He apparently found it important to include that dichotomy in his lectures, and I was loving it. As I was working through things in my heart and trying to figure out where I stood concerning Calvinism, this felt like a Godsend. Dare I say, through God's sovereignty, it appeared that He had me exactly where He wanted me to be during that stage of my journey.

I held on to Dr. Biermann's every word. I devoured the readings: books, articles, and the like. In addition to the lectures themselves, I absorbed as much as I could from the questions other students would ask the professor. After all, they were familiar with Lutheran thought far more than I was. I analyzed the dialogue between students as they engaged one another on the questions Dr. Biermann threw out there. I was firing on all cylinders; I could not afford to miss a thing. I even prioritized adequate sleep so I could be fully alert during class. Minimizing my cram time was the goal. **I was hungry for the truth, and by the grace of God, I was going to find it—or shall I say, it was finding me.**

AFTER MY BIERMANN IMPACT

By this point, I was now thinking about my music. Now that I was opening my mind to these ideas that were new to me but familiar to the ancient Church, I couldn't help but wonder how this would impact my art. Knowing myself, I would not feel comfortable hiding my shift in theology if it were to go that way. My personality wouldn't allow me to be Lutheran in secret but Reformed Baptist to the public. These thoughts were certainly budding, although I had not committed myself to Lutheran theology yet.

The more I learned, the more I would discuss with those in my circle. I didn't discuss matters with any deep conviction; I simply raised questions and asked my friends what they thought about things. I'm sure there were times I explained things wrongly or was unclear in my explanation since I was still trying to wrap my mind around it all. What I found fascinating was the contrast between what I was learning in school and what I was hearing across the pulpit at my local church.

Obviously, there were some similarities with what my local Reformed church was teaching. Yet I started to notice the differences in how the Christian life was discussed between the two. One of the fundamental differences was the Lutheran horizontal emphasis on serving neighbor as the place one lives out sanctification or vocation rather than the Reformed vertical focus on doing things for God.

Another noticeable contrast was the number of times we celebrated the Lord's Supper, or Communion. Students at school said they celebrated the Lord's Supper every Sunday. At my church, we took Communion once a month. Not only that, but we also saw it as a metaphor pointing back to what Jesus did long ago. I even remember my pastor at the time being careful to mention that "we do not believe Jesus is bodily present in the bread or the wine. This is only a memorial meal that Jesus told us to do to remember what He went through for us."

Although I was not committed to the Lutheran way at the time, I remember noticing how easily Jesus' words were redefined. My wheels were turning. I couldn't help but engage in my mind the things I was being confronted with in class. I thought, *But my professor made a good point recalling that Jesus says, "This bread is My body," and "This wine is My blood."* Then the Reformed Baptist rubber band in my mind would snap me back into place, and I'd conclude that the Lutheran idea was just weird and seemed impossible.

How can God be in those elements? *That's just weird and spooky*, I thought. The thing that was difficult to shake off, however, was the grammatical arguments for the Lutheran interpretation of Scripture. They presented a robust argument in class and in the readings, and I knew better than to so easily dismiss it. **Again, I was careful to move slowly.**

CHAPTER 8

LUTHERAN OUT LOUD

An additional emphasis that stood out to me was Confession and Absolution. Students and professors alike talked about this as if it were a normal thing to think about. I'd heard of Confession before, but *Absolution* wasn't a normal term used in the Reformed or generic American Evangelical space. It's normally associated with Roman Catholics. By and large, most of the Reformed persons I knew didn't pay much attention to Rome or speak of their brotherhood in a favorable way, unfortunately. For that reason, the very notion of Absolution is frowned upon.

I was learning that Lutherans did not practice Absolution in the same manner as Rome. There was no penance or extra practices to perform to assist in repentance. Yet the Lutherans were keen on preserving Absolution based on Scripture. I noticed the major difference while actually experiencing it myself. One of my minors was in counseling. We were given an assignment to actually see a counselor on staff at the seminary. At first, I was a bit put off by the idea, but I quickly resolved that it couldn't hurt.

The counselor and I met together for about four sessions, and things evolved relatively quickly due to how well our personalities worked together. While in one of the sessions, I was able to open up and confess my sin to a trained pastoral counselor. As we were ending the session, the counselor asked me if he could absolve me. I told him I was only familiar with the concept vaguely but was open to it. He asked if I would mind removing my hat. I said, "Not at all."

He then placed his hand on my head, stated my full name, and said something akin to, "In the place and by the command of Jesus Christ, my Lord, I forgive you all your sins in the name of the Father, the Son, and of the Holy Spirit." **After that experience, I nearly wept. It was such a personal and impactful one.** To have the forgiveness of sin pronounced over me in this unique way was indeed divine. I left the office in full confidence and assurance of the Lord's forgiveness.

As mentioned, confession of sin is commonplace among many believers. Yet most accountability groups are a time for sharing hard things with one another, followed by encouragement and some form of the Law given to try harder next time mixed with some practical steps toward detecting triggers and preventive measures. These are all good and right things. However, most people leave without the biblical comfort of Absolution. It's crucial that one hears the Absolution of the Lord by the one in His stead. **Not only does this bring forgiveness but it also reminds us that we are not saved by our performance or level of personal piety but by Jesus and His merits alone.**

Confession and Absolution takes place privately but also corporately. As the saints gather for Divine Service, immediately upon entrance, parishioners participate in Confession and Absolution. Out loud, they confess that they are sinners and have sinned. There's even a quiet time for private confession unto the

Lord. Then the pastor declares the forgiveness of sin over God's children, and they are absolved. There is literal Gospel happening all throughout the Divine Service. From the moment of entrance to the moment of departure. There's Confession and Absolution. The reading of God's Word. The singing of God's Word. The hearing of God's preached Word. Both Law and Gospel. This culminates in the Lord's Supper: the visible Word of God whereby Jesus is bodily present in the bread and wine. There's prayer, the sign of the cross is made, and before everyone makes an exit, they are reminded again that their sins are forgiven.

OVERCOMING THE FEELING OF BETRAYAL

After hearing of these things myself, I wanted to visit a Lutheran Church for the first time. But there was a colossal barrier to overcome: the personal accusation of disloyalty. There's an emotional and psychological component that I had to confront. I was extremely nervous, and I was still a bit skeptical and felt like I was turning my back on everyone. There was a sense of guilt that I could not ignore.

Those feelings are connected to your history with those you love dearly, who handed Christianity down to you. I could not help but think about family, former professors from my Reformed Baptist training, pastors and lay leaders whom I gleaned so much from, and long-term friends who had been with me every step of my journey. Last but not least, I thought of those who had supported my music for so long. If I took this step and actually visited this Lutheran church—what if I liked it? What if I found it to be a more accurate representation of Scripture? Then what? It was like hearing a thousand voices in my head all at once. Accusing voices, telling me to stay loyal to all these people who had impacted my faith.

Nonetheless, I decided that I would push through. **I had come this far and was loving what I was being exposed to. I could not unsee it.** I could not ignore Scripture and the way it was reshaping my thinking. I could not dismiss the well-reasoned arguments from Scripture and Church history that challenged my understanding of things. I decided, in my heart of hearts, that I was being compelled by the Holy Spirit to visit, and I could not betray my conscience. Off I went to search for a nearby confessional Lutheran church.

VISITING MY FIRST LUTHERAN CHURCH

Finally, Sunday arrived and I was heading to step foot, for the first time, in a Lutheran church building. I, at one point, literally laughed out loud. *What in the heck are you doing, FLAME?* After a little pep talk with myself, I entered in. On the inside, I found humans. Humans with hair and clothing and children. They could talk and sing. They even had shoes on and read from the same Bible as I did. I thought, *Maybe these creatures aren't that alien after all.*

As we made our way through liturgy, which in simple terms is the order of service, we began to sing from a book called a hymnal. I had no idea how to follow along. I could not find the song. The words skipped all over the pages, and I had to chase them around the box to stay on track. The first verse ends and picks back up the third line down on the bottom right of the next page. It was embarrassing. Good thing I have a mean mumble that almost sounds like words. Though I didn't know the melody either; I just did more pretending and smiling until the song was over. I survived, and no one knew. I was filled with pride.

Besides that, I loved it! They even had a portion during liturgy where the children came to the front and heard a short sermon from the pastor, all while the adults were still in the room. It's like the children were valued equally. I had never seen such a thing outside of youth programs that featured kids or teens on a special occasion. As I left, I thought to myself, *That wasn't bad at all.* I was eager to visit more Lutheran churches.

As time progressed and I was making my way through seminary, I was really narrowing down on my Lutheran leanings. For this reason, I decided that I would only release music that spoke in generalities concerning Christianity. I didn't want to release songs in my typical teaching style while I was in limbo. I thought it best while in this transitional season to hold off from speaking too soon on what I was learning. I had not fully committed in my heart to it, but I was becoming more and more certain that I did not want to communicate the doctrines of the Reformed Church any longer.

In a healthy way, I'd argue, I was losing the ability to track down my former way of processing the faith from the Scriptures. I was undergoing a paradigm shift. Too much was at stake. I wasn't emotionally attached to the three songs I released during that time. They were sonically pleasing and received well, for the most part. But I knew I had more to come. Things were brewing, and I was patiently waiting before the big reveal.

Graduation was approaching quickly. Wow, where did two years go? I enrolled in 2016 as a frightened student gasping for breath, and now I was near graduation in 2018 feeling sturdy. I remember on graduation day, one of my professors asked me jokingly, "Are you Lutheran yet?"

I chuckled and said, "Maybe. I'm still thinking it through. I think so, but I'm not sure."

We laughed. I decided the best way forward was to take some time after graduation to further process things outside of the academic environment. I didn't want the social pressure to influence my decision.

That time after graduation turned into one year. It took me an entire year before I made my resolve to theologically align myself with confessional Lutheranism. I studied and prayed. Prayed and studied. I asked plenty of questions of those I trusted. I had great dialogue and exchange with brilliant minds outside the Lutheran space. I was convinced. The things I was exposed to during graduate school were certainly in the text of Scripture. I was now ready to go on record with full conviction. I considered deeply the consequences and resolved to see my decision through. No matter what it would cost me.

The important thing to me was that, ironically, although Lutherans bear Luther's name, Lutheranism is not about Martin Luther supremacy. The name *Lutheran* was given to those who were in support of him during his excommunication. As my friend says, if someone in the hood gives you a nickname, it sticks. You are forced to go by that name, most likely, whether you like it or not. When I moved to Louisville, Kentucky, for a time, I had to find a new barber. When I finally found one, he asked me my name and where I was from. I told him I was from St. Louis, Missouri. From that day forward, whenever I came to the shop, he would say, "What's good, St. Louis?!" Needless to say, my name became St. Louis to everyone else who worked there. So those seeking to slight Luther and his supporters gave the name *Lutheran* to those pupils and, well, here we are.

Here are Luther's own words as it relates to people being identified by him and his name:

> In the first place, I ask that men make no reference to my name; let them call themselves Christians, not Lutherans. What is Luther? After all, the teaching is not mine [John 7:16]. Neither was I crucified for anyone [1 Cor. 1:13]. St. Paul, in 1 Corinthians 3, would not allow the Christians to call themselves Pauline or Petrine, but Christian. How then should I—poor stinking maggot-fodder that I am—come to have men call the children of Christ by my wretched name? Not so, my dear friends; let us abolish all party names and call ourselves Christians, after him whose teaching we hold. The papists deservedly have a party name, because they are not content with the teaching and name of Christ, but want to be papist as well. Let them be papist then, since the pope is their master. I neither am nor want to be anyone's master. I hold, together with the universal church, the one universal teaching of Christ, who is our only master [Matt. 23:8].[4]

I say amen to Luther. Still, nicknames, or in this case intended derogatory names, stick too. In keeping with the theme of names, I anticipated some name-calling upon exposing people to my shift in doctrine. I could even picture the specific people I imagined would

---

4   Martin Luther, *Luther's Works*, American Edition, vol. 45 (Philadelphia: Fortress Press, 1962), 70–71.

be the most taken back and hostile. Nevertheless, I had removed people's opinions from the throne of my heart and resolved to be authentic to what God had wrought in my life.

RETHINKING MISCONCEPTIONS

I was renewed. I was rejuvenated. It was as if God opened the windows of heaven and poured out blessings of joy. Blessings of peace. Blessings of assurance. This was particularly important to me because, for eighteen years, I relinquished the simplicity of the Christian faith. I grew accustomed to mental gymnastics to explain or explain away the plain meaning of the text. Whether well intended or not, all deviations from the straightforward and clear representation of Scripture will only add the burden and weight of the Law. Through God's kindness, the vocation of Luther, and Lutheran thought, I now knew the peace God promised through His Good News earned by Christ's merits.

I had wrongfully exchanged the reality that Jesus died for the sin of the world. I trained my eye to see a crucifixion only for a select few. In doing so, I stripped myself of the assurance God established in the giving of His Son for me. For us. When frantically asking, "Am I one of the persons Jesus died for?" I should have been able to say, "Yes!" and to draw relief from the truth that He died for us all and that by faith, *anyone can come*. The tango I settled for caused me to dance between resting in Jesus' finished work on the cross and doing more for God to affirm that I was one of the select few.

Another change in my mindset came from how I saw statements such as "getting closer to God," "more of God," "glorifying

God," and "going deeper in Christ" went from the innocence of what they are intended to mean to shorthand for more Law-keeping *for* God. Obviously, the key phrase here is "for God." Now, all my behavior modification or obedience, sacrificial living, and skill sets are directed toward people. To make their lives less burdensome. To enhance their joy. To love them for their sake. Yes, growing out of God's work in me. Yes, informed by God's rubric of right and wrong. Yes, with His desires in mind. Yes, always frail and falling short. But not to earn extra credit from Him or to prove myself. Besides, can we really do anything for God?

I love how God makes this clear in Psalm 50:12:

> If I were hungry, I would not tell you, for the world
> and its fullness are Mine.

This passage always makes me laugh. I picture God saying this to someone. I imagine Him giving them full eye contact with laughter in His eyes and gesturing His hands to point at everything in sight.

Not only that, but it makes me laugh knowing how true it is. He literally owns everything. If for one nanosecond He had a need, He has every single thing at His disposal. There would be no need for Him to tell us or ask us for anything: not our attention, time, money, or praise. Jesus picks up on this theme in Luke 19:39–40:

> And some of the Pharisees in the crowd said
> to Him, "Teacher, rebuke Your disciples." He
> answered, "I tell you, if these were silent, the very
> stones would cry out."

This further proves God can do what He wants and will get what He wants. He is not lonely or in desperate need of attention and worship from His human creation. He is not discontent, unsatisfied, and sitting around in His omnipresence, waiting on us humans to get serious about Him so we can work for Him. Not at all. **He is the eternal, infinite, content Creator who allows His human subjects to share in His work and to participate in the story He is telling through human history. What a privilege.**

As I began to experience a reshaping of my understanding of God and His character, I could not put new wine into old wineskins. Or to say it differently, my understanding of God could no longer be contained in former catchphrases that I once held dear. For example, Question 1 from the *Westminster Shorter Catechism* says, "Man's chief end is to glorify God and to enjoy him for ever."[5] I'm not saying there's nothing good about this statement. However, I no longer see this as God's ultimate goal for humanity. It sounds great, but what does it really mean? It can lead to more questions than it does to more clarity.

How do you determine when a person is actually accomplishing that end? Is it a certain amount of prayers? A certain length of prayers? Is it sharing your faith with twenty or one hundred people per week? Is it only watching PG-rated movies or one R-rated movie but with Christian themes? How much enjoyment in God are we talking about? Is it the type of enjoyment a kid has in the candy store or the amount that a newly married couple has on the first night of the honeymoon? Again, the statement sounds great, but when you push on it, it leads to more questions and causes one to chase a moving target.

---

5   The Westminster Shorter Catechism of the Westminster Assembly (1648).

Chasing that moving target causes one to focus on the vertical more than the horizontal. The vertical describes our relationship with God. From a Calvinist perspective, this is typically lived out with a person looking deep within themselves to detect their degree of joy in Christ, their measure of enjoyment in the things of God. For example, how much are you enjoying your ministry or volunteer time at the homeless shelter? Then you begin to heavily monitor your motives. Why am I really doing this? Am I doing this for praise and attention, so as to appear more holy? Or am I really doing it for God's glory?

This pits the horizontal against the vertical. The horizontal is how we interact with those around us. To do something simply for the sake of one's neighbor seems less holy. We'd feel better saying we are doing it "for God." Don't hear me wrong. Yes, we do work as unto the Lord, but this does not mean we have to be buried subterranean levels down, introspecting into our souls. We do not have to examine our deepest thoughts to ensure that we have more motives on the scale tipping God's way as opposed to the person we are serving. In fact, this is how Jesus describes it—we should be so lost in serving people around us that we are unaware that by serving them, we actually served Him too. Matthew 25:34–40 makes this clear.

> Then the King will say to those on His right,
> "Come, you who are blessed by My Father, inherit
> the kingdom prepared for you from the foundation
> of the world. For I was hungry and you gave Me
> food, I was thirsty and you gave Me drink, I was a
> stranger and you welcomed Me, I was naked and

you clothed Me, I was sick and you visited Me, I was in prison and you came to Me." Then the righteous will answer Him, saying, "Lord, when did we see You hungry and feed You, or thirsty and give You drink? And when did we see You a stranger and welcome You, or naked and clothe you? And when did we see You sick or in prison and visit You?" And the King will answer them, "Truly, I say to you, as you did it to one of the least of these My brothers, you did it to Me."

They were so consumed by living out their faith and sacrificially serving those in need that they hadn't processed that, by caring for others, they were simultaneously serving Jesus. To say it again, plainly: we serve Jesus by serving others.

Here's another perspective I learned. In the Calvinist circle I ran in, the concern was that one would make an idol out of created things. Therefore, in order to guard against that, one should be hyperfocused on doing things with the highest of motivations to God's glory alone. This, in my estimation, leads to a low view of creation. God's good creation often gets caught in the crossfire. It can even appear to function as a barrier between truly glorifying God and worshiping the thing created rather than the Creator, to use the apostle Paul's words in Romans 1:25. For instance, someone I know posted a picture on social media of the beach. The caption boasted of the beauty in the landscape—the seemingly endless body of water rippling with waves. The soft white sand. The sun blazing as the seagulls gracefully soared across the skies. And then out of nowhere, the person quickly said, "Yeah, this stuff looks good, but it ain't nothing compared to my God and His beauty! This world don't mean nothing to me! God made it all!"

Okay, wow! Why was bruh mad at the beach? My estimation of his inner conflict was that he felt like he had to be angry in order to properly reorient his thoughts and motivations. His theology was informing his affections, and his affections quickly alerted his mood: **Regroup! Regroup! You are about to make an idol out of the beach! Danger, danger! He didn't want it to come across as if he were glorifying the beach more than the God of the beach.** This is an unfortunate reflex that is carved into this way of thinking, and I know it all too well myself.

In 2005, I wrote a song that appeared on my second album. In the lyrics, I made this statement:

> *I don't ask how many albums I sold*
> *because honestly*
> *I really don't want to know.*
> *See what I wanna know is*
> *from what I wrote*
> *is it grabbing a soul*
> *into the truth*
> *of the fact that He rose.*

Although this was a deep, true, and genuine sentiment, it is unfortunately misguided. Furthermore, I didn't just say the lines in the song, I lived them. I actually did not care nor did I do the responsible thing and monitor my business affairs the way I should have.

I thought God would be more pleased if I neglected "worldly things" like record sales and money and focused vehemently more on sharing the Gospel and communicating sound doctrine, which in my mind was exclusively Reformed Baptist teachings. Out of all the hands that a project has to pass through before it is released to the public, not one person noticed or felt the need to address that line of thinking. I'm not blaming them at all. My point is to say that this type of reasoning is commonplace and the expectation of a Christian artist—or person, for that matter—who is really serious about Jesus.

Later, a true friend of mine (who was not a five-point Calvinist) did make mention of that line and said, "FLAME, I know you love Jesus, but you also need to check on your album sales. That, too, is pleasing to God." Being fully convinced of my stance, I dismissed him and his advice as worldly, unfortunately. We laugh about it today.

Reasons like these are why I say there's an inherent temptation written into the fabric of my former tradition to have a lower view of creation. When the focus is primarily on affections, heart motivations, and performing good deeds with a vertical incentive, then things below get summed up as a threat to holiness, an ever-looming trap leading to the doorsteps of the idol-making factory.

Even in Luther's day, this was a common theme. It was taught that if you were to abandon your family life and join the monastery to become a monk or the nunnery to become a nun, then you were doing the more "holy" thing. Leaving family, material riches, and possessions behind to commit your life to church work was esteemed higher. One was deemed more spiritual and pious in the hierarchy of Christendom. Luther pointed out that God calls us all to serve according to His will. (See Ephesians 2:10.) Under the guidance of the Holy Spirit, Solomon was right when he said there's nothing new under the sun. Age-old ideas are repackaged in a contemporary context. May we be ever vigilant to guard against this pretending to be the way of Christianity.

TIME FOR NEW LUTHERAN MUSIC

It was time! I was finally ready to reapproach my music in the fashion I'm most naturally drawn to—teaching, connecting dots, analyzing, and building a case. The idea for my next album started for me during one of my classes when I heard the phrase *extra nos* used. The professor explained that it was a Latin phrase that means "outside of us." As he continued to expand on its meaning and use, it was as if more oxygen was entering my brain, leading to my heart. God-breathed, faith-sustaining oxygen. From then onward, I was hooked. Similar to Luther's paradigm-shifting experience while reading Romans, I, too, was gripped by the notion that what God is doing for us is outside of us.

This idea shadowed me everywhere I went. I could not break away from it. It constantly led me to God's promise and bid me rest in what God was doing for me as opposed to my own efforts. Not even my joint efforts with God would suffice, thus freeing me to work for my family, friends, and for all from the freedom in Christ. For this reason, I titled my first project, after six months of silence, *Extra Nos*. Not only did I want to provide a clear contrast between Lutheran thought and Reformed thought but also to help liberate many that I knew personally and those influenced by me over the years. Calvin served us well in many regards, but I wanted those who subscribe to my platform to also be exposed to helpful things from the Scriptures and the Lutheran tradition that Calvin and his followers unfortunately punted.

One of the important ideas to communicate with this short project was the two kinds, or types, of righteousness: 2KR, for short. On the interlude of the project "Good Works," I made this statement:

Man, I love how Luther
emphasized that God doesn't need our good works,
but our neighbor does.
I mean, that's so weighty when you think about it
because all our good deeds,
our sanctification, our skill sets,
and responsibilities in various roles
are for the benefit of those around us.
Our families, society, our neighbor, right?
But what makes us right with God,
Paul says, is our faith.
That's how we are made righteous
and how we remain righteous: in Christ.
But when you blur those lines
and start looking at your sanctification
for assurance that you are right with God,
a bunch of problems arise.
First off, we end up filled with discouragement
from constantly missing the mark.

We can also end up filled with self-doubt
from constantly applying subjective and
arbitrary measures
to assess our level of sanctification
in order to determine whether or not we are justified.
Or on the flip side,
we can be filled with self-righteousness
as a result of fulfilling some criteria we created
and then, in turn, cast judgment on others
who don't check our specific boxes.
This is a common experience,
especially among Calvinists (Reformed Baptists,
in my experience)
because it flows from functionally placing sanctification
above justification.
This stems from the fact that, in general,
for Calvinists, there is a primary emphasis
on Godward obedience to the Law,
which perpetuates this inward focus.
Luther, on the other hand,
places the perfect work of God in justification
over the incomplete process of sanctification.
We are to look extra nos, or outside of ourselves,
toward the righteousness of faith,
which is our justification, for assurance.
This is where we find identity, stability,
objectivity, and security.

Luther is committed to justification truly being sola fide, meaning by faith alone.

His primary emphasis is on serving your neighbor through your vocation.

This emphasis helps to maintain the clear distinction between our identity being found in our righteousness of faith,

which we receive from God, a.k.a. passive righteousness, versus our performance, or our active righteousness, which is righteousness we live out for the benefit of our neighbor.

As Christians, we should seek both kinds of righteousness, but for different purposes.

We should guard against our good works becoming the basis for our righteousness before God.

And we should guard against our righteousness of faith being used to eliminate the need for good works.

Our good works have value here on earth, coram mundo.

But this does not justify us before God, coram Deo.

It is vital that we keep these separate!

This sums it up. However, I will highlight a few portions I hope will prove to be helpful. This statement is important:

But when you blur those lines and start looking at your sanctification for assurance that you are right with God, a bunch of problems arise. First off, we end up filled with discouragement from constantly missing the mark. We can also end up filled with self-doubt from constantly

applying subjective and arbitrary measures to assess our level of sanctification in order to determine whether or not we are justified. Or on the flip side, we can be filled with self-righteousness as a result of fulfilling some criteria we created and then, in turn, cast judgment on others who don't check our specific boxes.

It's been said that misunderstanding or ignoring the two kinds of righteousness will only lead to one of two outcomes: a person will either be filled with pride or despair. That's it. Personally, the way I'm wired, I'm less likely to dance with pride, though I'm not exempt from her invitation to tango. If you're like me, you're probably less likely to make a big deal about yourself, your accomplishments, or your possessions. There isn't much fulfillment in that. Besides, who wants all that attention anyway? No, thanks. Yet persons like us can easily fall into despair. We apparently have a heightened sense of inadequacies and can be drawn into a pit of sadness more easily. Not feeling good enough. Prone to discouragement.

This can turn to pride's B side. Side A would be an expanded appetite for outward acknowledgment, attention, and praise, concluding that one is superior to others. Side B to pride would be hyperfocusing on yourself in a reclusive way—withholding yourself and your talents, and not sacrificing for the sake of others. Also, this side of pride is prone to not believe God's words of promise but rather to trust in your own inner word, gripping you and gridlocking your emotional bandwidth from physically serving others, concluding that your feelings or discomfort are supreme.

I believe God's good expression in diverse human personalities displays itself in those who are comfortable leading and confident in their abilities to work hard and do a good job as well as those who have a heightened sense of themselves and reserve their energy for specific people and tasks. They analyze, calculate, count the cost, and then strike with precision before they "put themselves out there."

Nonetheless, we cannot blur the lines between our righteousness that we live out before one another or before the world (which is what the Latin phrase *coram mundo* means) with the righteousness that we passively receive from God (which is what the Latin phrase *coram Deo* means: "before God"). If we do, we will functionally fall into the trap of either "if only my meager deeds were good enough, maybe God would accept me," which leads to discouragement and despair, or "my deeds are immaculate and I have earned God's favor based on my high-quality performance," thus leading to pride and self-deception.

I've found that Christians who are high functioning, very disciplined, and who were given a lot of structure during their childhood excel at performance of any sort. They don't necessarily believe their high aptitude in behavior and morals will earn them salvation; for them, it's mostly a challenge to not look at "struggling Christians" as lesser-than, lazy, or filled with excuses. This is where the other portion comes into play, which says, "we can be filled with self-righteousness as a result of fulfilling some criteria we created and then, in turn, cast judgment on others who don't check our specific boxes."

In other words, they express things like, "*I'm* reading my Bible every day, even on days I don't feel like it. Why can't he do the same?" Or they'll say things like, "I just don't understand how someone can still be struggling with the same drug addiction for so long. Haven't they been a Christian for five years now?" In their minds, they've created a target for others to hit based on their personal aptitude, and they hold them to a standard that they've created. This allows them to feel better, more accomplished, and more holy than the struggler.

In reality, what's most likely going on is that they've simply lowered the bar in some other area of life and have convinced themselves that they aren't that bad. It's like a person bragging to others that they've slam-dunked a basketball in the hoop, but they actually lowered the hoop and the basket was for kids. God's standards are too high for us to slam the ball or get a perfect score. His standard is perfection.

James 2:10:

> For whoever keeps the whole law but fails in one
> point has become guilty of all of it.

In terms of what makes us right with God, you scoring ninety-nine out of one hundred is the same losing outcome as scoring zero in God's estimation. This is for the Christian and non-Christian alike, for the new Christian and the mature believer who's been living in faith for thirty years and counting. From the starting point, the dash in between, and the ending point, a person is only made right with God because of Jesus. Jesus' incarnation, sinless life, death on the cross, and resurrection are the only basis upon which God allows a person into His family, into His heaven. Period.

By faith, we simply trust in the finished work of Jesus' life and work for the benefits of what Jesus earned for us.

Yes, this saving faith in Christ expresses itself in new obedience: Acts of service and kindness. Pursuits of purity and moral growth. Giving of time and talent and talking to others about the Gospel. Nevertheless, none of those good things will earn you extra credit in God's mind. Nor will they contribute to your entrance into God's heaven. And when you fall short of upholding those good things that are consistent with God's desired way, because you will, you can confess your sin, receive absolution, and turn toward doing the right thing the next time.

My next statement deserves some attention and clarity. As it relates to blurring the lines between our spiritual growth and how to be on God's good side eternally, I state, "This is a common experience, especially among Calvinists (Reformed Baptists, in my experience), because it flows from functionally placing sanctification above justification. This stems from the fact that, in general, for Calvinists, there is a primary emphasis on Godward obedience to the Law, which perpetuates this inward focus."

Obviously, John Calvin himself and those who continued his movement were in agreement with Luther, their predecessor through whom they drew their understanding, on justification by faith alone. I am not accusing Calvin or Calvinists of teaching works-based salvation. Neither am I accusing them of teaching that we are saved based on God's work plus a little bit of our cooperation and contribution as well. Hence my intentional use of the word *functionally*.

What I mean is this: on paper or on a test, when a Calvinist is asked, "Are we saved by faith alone?" they would answer correctly, "Yes." If asked, "Do you add or contribute anything to your salvation by your spiritual growth?" The Reformed would correctly answer, "No." They'd be right. However, the way progressive sanctification is positioned in preaching, the literature, and practical application, can and has caused many to stumble. In all fairness, there are things in every camp that can and have caused many to stumble. Yet my point here is to explain my experience and how I was lifted from this particular stumbling. When a person is regularly challenged to "make your calling and election sure" beyond the scriptural scope or intended meaning of that passage (2 Peter 1:10), one grows accustomed to doubting one's faith and election.

When persons are regularly told they must be "feeling" joy toward God, they grow used to focusing on Godward obedience, which expresses itself in looking within to find pure motives, thoughts, and feelings. When being told to examine themselves to see if they are of the faith, again, beyond the biblical scope and immediate context of that specific passage and circumstance, this coaches members to let doubt fester.

As people are more than occasionally cautioned that they may hear from Jesus, "depart from Me, for I never knew you," they will as a direct consequence become consumed by anxiety, especially if they are wired to be more prone to despair. What also adds to the confusion is when you preach in such a way that makes the main thrust of Christianity to be about killing sin so that sin does not kill you. Yes, we ought to be ever renewed and growing more accustomed to living for others as opposed to ourselves. However, the focus should be on serving neighbor and not hunting sin, which again leads to more internal focus.

I believe people will be better served if you help them understand how to live life on earth for the sake of making life better for others and themselves, as unto the Lord, not primarily out of fear of "falling from grace," losing your heavenly rewards, or "being given over to a seared conscience" (in other words, a "reprobate mind"). For example, if a Christian couple is having issues and one spouse is applying the most relationship-hindering pressure, then the focus should be on getting help to better serve the other partner. This is not primarily out of fear that sin is going to kill you. Getting help is an act of love toward your neighbor. In this way, you are serving Jesus and you serve your spouse. Based on Matthew 25:37–40, can't you hear Jesus saying, "When I was being neglected, you turned toward Me"? You'll say, "When did I see You neglected, Lord, and turn toward You?" And our Christ would say, "When you sought help to love on your spouse, you were loving, serving, and turning toward Me." Selah.

The subtle difference is in the direction of the focus. The horizontal focus directs you to live for neighbor. It frees you to be present "on the ground," fully engaged in the matters of life. You are free to be present mentally, emotionally, and practically, lending all your creative and nurturing attention to the relationship. In this way, the spouses are learning to care for one another's needs and quirks as opposed to being motivated by fear of losing salvation or being preoccupied with trying to have joy before the Lord as an expression of doing things with the right motivations. That unnatural internal focus blurs the lines and leads a person within as opposed to without.

FLAME LEFT CHRISTIANITY

So far, does everything I'm saying sound Christian? I'd hope your answer is yes because it is. Well, not everybody thought so. Some still do not believe so to this day, as I am typing this. When some people saw that my *Extra Nos* EP cover art was in the ancient Christian art form of iconography, many raised their eyebrows. One person texted me immediately and thought I was claiming to be Jesus Himself. I was like, "Really? What led you to believe such an odd thing?"

He said, "You are depicted with a robe and have a halo behind your head. That represents Jesus, right? Or, at least that's how I've seen Him illustrated in most pictures." I laughed. Then I explained that the cover art was not my reveal-as-the-Messiah announcement but simply a style of art devout Christians have used throughout the ages to depict Christians, biblical scenes, and figures. I assured him that he could relax.

Next, once the project released, I was made aware that there were a few Facebook groups created to discuss me becoming Roman Catholic. To which I thought, *Roman Catholic? When did I say that? I'm not Roman Catholic; I'm confessional Lutheran. Did they even listen to the project?* People went on and on about how I'd abandoned "sound doctrine" for the teachings that nearly destroyed Christianity. I can only imagine the "prayer air traffic" as they lamented and sent up countless prayers to the Lord that He would lead me back to the truth, that I would turn from heresy and back to Calvinism, the "true exposition of Scripture," as they'd say.

Don't get me wrong, I sense the love in the misguided prayer request. The fact that people would go out of their way to create a Facebook thread dedicated to me and the state of my salvation is coated in love. Yet the filling on the inside of the love-coated prayers was misinformation. It would have been better to love me by at least accurately listening and acknowledging what my theological change was, as opposed to assuming or guessing based on little attention given to my actual words.

One guy contacted a dear friend of mine and asked, "What's wrong with FLAME? Is he okay?"

"Nothing's wrong; why do you ask that?" my friend inquired.

"He's Lutheran now. When most people make such a dramatic shift in their thinking or theology, something must really be wrong," the guy replied.

My homie sternly replied, "Nah, bruh, you got FLAME wrong. If he became Lutheran, it was after much research, prayer, and deep consideration. He's not a hasty dude."

I'm grateful for good friends who hold you down even when you're not around to defend yourself. He was right. There was nothing quick about me becoming Lutheran in my theological framework.

This next story is hilarious to me. I cannot make this stuff up. Another guy reached out and told me his church was celebrating the five-hundred-year anniversary of Luther's Reformation and the nailing of the Ninety-Five Theses to the Castle Church door. He also mentioned that many of them consider me an apostate now that I've become Lutheran. He said, "Wait. How are we celebrating Martin Luther and his contribution to Christianity while in the same breath we are condemning FLAME to eternal fire for being Lutheran?" I guess they had never really thought about it. We laughed.

Just recently, at the time of this writing, a person attempted to "cancel" me. I'm assuming this person was of some notoriety, although I confess I didn't give the time or attention to research him or the size of his following. He sent out a public service announcement to all those under his influence to have nothing to do with FLAME because FLAME now believes what Lutherans believe. Danger! Danger! So wait, since I'm no longer Reformed Baptist, I have departed from Christianity and should be avoided at all costs? Wow! Curious.

I admit that I'm not too terribly shocked because while I was in that space, I had a very narrow understanding of who was saved and who was not. I recall listening to a debate held by a popular Reformed Baptist apologist titled "Are Roman Catholics Our Brothers?" In the debate, the general conclusion from the Reformed person was that we should at least be gravely skeptical because, ultimately, they have a different Gospel. That was a pretty commonplace stance concerning Roman Catholics from what I gathered during my eighteen years in that space. "We judge each Roman Catholic person and parish case by case," many would say. So it was with the Eastern Church too. That is, if they ever came up.

When I released a song titled "We Gon' Reign" about the persecuted church, I dedicated it to the twenty-one Coptic Christians who were kidnapped and beheaded on a beach in Libya in 2015.

I was nervous because I knew many in my circle did not consider them believers. There is a similar sentiment concerning those who are from the Arminian spectrum of doctrine as well. Though most would not outright say they are not brothers and sisters in the faith, the prevailing attitude toward them is pity and skepticism. This negative disposition concerning those outside the Reformed space was rampant.

It must be said: I am not innocent either. There is blood on my hands too, I confess. For years, I was a part of conversations about who was really saved and who wasn't based on whether their theology closely matched ours. Or we would judge if their sanctification was Ivy-League level or community-college level or, perhaps, simply college-dropout level. We were masters at judging fruit, determining if a person's moral and theological performance met our checklist. If so, we considered the person "solid." If not, we'd at least do the courtesy of saying that the person is a "professing Christian," meaning they say they are with their lips but, based on our estimation, we were skeptical and could not vouch for them.

A classic I've heard from some is this: "FLAME must have never understood Calvinism in the first place." It feels like a script some have read from whenever I hear it or see it in my comment section online. To which I reply, "Well, if I never understood it, what does it say that for eighteen years of my teaching it publicly, rapping didactically about it in the span of nine albums, being featured on many other Reformed rapper's projects, teaching classes, speaking at hundreds and hundreds of events, and acquiring a bachelor's degree through rigorous training at arguably one of the finest Reformed Bible colleges that no one ever accused me then of not understanding Calvinism?" It's only when I say that I now disagree with it as a systematic theology that, all of a sudden, I must have never understood it in the first place. Again, this is through years of intense study, comparing and contrasting, prayer, and conversation. Certainly not a haphazard decision. It's hard for many to accept that I can no longer with a good conscience pretend that I see Calvinism taught in the whole of Scripture. There are aspects that I still agree with, but those would be things most Christians would affirm even outside of the Reformation tradition.

Truthfully, I have compassion on many because it took me three years of studying Christianity as it's been preserved in Lutheran theology before I would embrace it. I experienced the full range of emotions that some are feeling now. The utter shock and disgust of Lutheran thought. The confusion as to what in the world Lutherans were even talking about. The skepticism to see if I was being deceived and being drawn into spooky and heretical doctrine. The curiosity and observation stage. The open mind to take the notions more seriously. The humbling acceptance that Lutherans may have a point. The forced grappling with what I could no longer argue with or unsee. The eventual compliance with what I could no longer deny. The necessary space to ward off hasty and anxious decision-making, so as to avoid buyer's remorse. The eventual return to fully lay hold of what the illumination of the Holy Spirit exposed and taught me from His Bible—which is, as I always say, ancient Christianity that has been preserved in Lutheran thought.

That elicits empathy in me, knowing that I am further along in my considerations and conclusions. **I realize these are shocking ideas to the ear of the generic American Christian. Most of** us have never been given the opportunity to ponder the faith beyond the contemporary take on things. We mostly get our ideas about Christianity from Sunday School at a family church as a kid; from Christian pop culture, music, and social media; from conversations with other people who claim to know a bit about the Bible; and from what we've read on our own in the Bible. That muddy mixture is mostly how we learned of our faith. I remember that my Church history timeline was as follows: the Bible days, whispers of Luther, Billy Graham, and then us. Later, I added Calvin next to Luther. I simply hadn't been exposed to the vast scope of Church history.

THE SACRAMENTS

For this reason, the closest I came to understanding something akin to what God does to save extra nos, outside of us, came from John Calvin. I'm thankful for Calvin and that he brought me to Luther, ultimately. Without traveling down the road of the Reformed, I would have never been more heavily exposed to the hidden treasure that is confessional Lutheranism. Through Lutheranism, I have been brought nearer to the purity of the Word of God itself. Thank You, Lord!

When I concluded that there was no more ground for me to walk on and that I had reached the end of the road, God removed the fog and showed me more path—a path leading to rest, hope, joy, and assurance of salvation. **Included in that discovery was the sweet and wonderful teaching of the Word of God and the visible Word of God, the Sacraments.**

Although it took a while, eventually, through much kicking and screaming, I began to see the Sacraments as tangible connections to the objective reality of what Jesus accomplished on the cross for sinners: forgiveness of sin. It is through Baptism that God applies His grace to needy people like ourselves. I am reminded of my Baptism as the location of my deliverance from darkness and placement into Christ Himself. It is through the bread and the wine at the Lord's Supper that I receive, in my mouth, the body and blood of my Savior for life and forgiveness.

Just as the Israelites knew that their sins were atoned for by the sacrifice and eating of the lamb, my assurance is found in the partaking of the Lord's Supper.

Matthew 26:26–28:

> Jesus took bread, and after blessing it broke it and
> gave it to the disciples, and said, "Take, eat; this
> is My body." And He took a cup, and when He had
> given thanks He gave it to them, saying, "Drink of
> it, all of you, for this is My blood of the covenant,
> which is poured out for many for the forgiveness
> of sins."

He and I become one as I, too, am united with all the saints who eat at the table of blessing.

I've never felt so armed against the flesh and the devil. In fact, feelings no longer lead the charge. They can ebb and flow as much as they want. No longer do I search for assurance in my ability to keep God's perfect standard. I do not rely on my mind's ability to drum up its best cognitive recall of what Jesus did for me and my proper mental appreciation and admiration of it. No longer am I threatened by adverbs asking if I "really," "genuinely," or "sincerely" believe. No longer am I confused by arbitrary measures to judge my performance on any given day.

I now look to His constant coming to me, to us, at the Lord's Table. Rooted in the wonderful work He accomplished in His life, death, and resurrection, I experience Him afresh as often as we sup with Him during the Divine Service. A few have said, "You never truly understood Calvinism in the first place." To this, I reply, "I believe the problem is that I understood it all too well and am now experiencing the joy of true *sola fide* that only exists in shadows elsewhere."

CHAPTER 9

CHRIST FOR YOU

The intensity of my rejoicing cannot be quenched because I remember the fright that accompanied the culture of Calvinism. God's wrath. Church discipline. Making your calling and election sure. These were overwhelmingly common emphases made during my time as a Reformed Baptist Calvinist. To overemphasize these matters beyond the textual scope is hazardous. Soul threatening. There were times I would let communion pass because I didn't feel worthy, afraid I would fall sick or die (see 1 Corinthians 11:30). I did not realize the "unworthy manner" wasn't my lack of worthiness but, according to Paul, not discerning Christ's body and blood in the bread and wine or to profane Christ's bodily presence in the Supper haphazardly in some manner or another.

1 Corinthians 11:29:

> For anyone who eats and drinks without discerning the body eats and drinks judgment on himself.

1 Corinthians 11:27:

> Whoever, therefore, eats the bread or drinks the cup of the Lord in an unworthy manner will be guilty concerning the body and blood of the Lord.

I thank God I have been rightly oriented! Now, I don't run from the Lord's Table to deal with my brokenness, but the complete opposite. I run to the Lord's Table to receive forgiveness.

Again, Matthew 26:26–28:

> "Take, eat; this is My body." And He took a cup,
> and when He had given thanks He gave it to them,
> saying, "Drink of it, all of you, for this is My blood
> of the covenant, which is poured out for many for
> the forgiveness of sins."

Right doctrine affects your worship. Your peace. And it stimulates good works.

For this reason, I wanted others to know the joy, forgiveness, and truth concerning the Lord's Supper. The next project I decided to release was titled *Christ for You*. Although dense, this was another short body of work with the goal of unpacking the matter of the Lord's Supper. The opening line of the EP says, "Maybe the reason you feel so empty is because you've reduced Christianity down to just a contemplative spirituality."

The intention and meaning behind this statement came from witnessing so many people become disillusioned with Christianity. According to many of them, Christianity was beginning to simply feel like a collection of doctrines that should be committed to memory and readily recalled. To add to that, many would say those doctrines only remind you of how bad you are and how distant from being good. The only remedy to that was yet again to remember and recall what Jesus did about that a long time ago, in the past.

Obviously, this is a grim take on things, but it is telling and springs from a good observation. Between a heavy emphasis on the necessity of a neat and tidy systematic understanding of doctrine and the Sacraments being reduced down to a metaphor, one can understand the disillusionment. That—coupled with a heavy dose of caution toward the mysteriousness and spontaneity of the Holy Spirit's workings—restricts you mostly to the mind, to pondering, thinking, reasoning, keeping logical consistency, and recalling.

Please don't hear me wrong, I am not downplaying these traits. They are all good gifts from God to help us engage one another and the world around us. They provide order and structure to thought, organization to ideas and observations, and clarity and understanding for interaction and communication. But to limit your Christian experience, by and large, to the cognitive and contemplative side of things is harmful. God did not create us as brains on a stick. He did not only create the natural world.

The world consists of visible and invisible realities. We are multifaceted beings meant to interact with the diversity of life. This is a challenge for the contemporary Christian person. We believe we must first understand a thing before we can accept it as true. The truth or reality of a thing is not based on whether you can understand it. Nor how well you can process it, wrap your mind around it, systematically categorize it, and explain it. Here, Luther's famous advice is helpful. We use logic and reason the way God intended, as a servant. Not a master.[6]

---

6 Martin Luther, *What Luther Says* (St. Louis: Concordia Publishing House, 1959), § 3733.

These things we humbly confess because God revealed them, not necessarily because we understand them:

- A triune God
- A God-man
- A virgin birth
- A book written by men but inspired by the Holy Spirit
- Jesus died for all.
- God alone saves.
- God desires all to be saved.
- Humans who resist their salvation bear the blame for their sinful resistance, not God. The devil shares in that blame.
- God elects for salvation, not damnation. Selah.
- Jesus will return to establish the new heaven and the new earth.

It is crucial to what it means to be a Christian to posture our hearts to embrace what God has revealed. We should ask God to work humility in our minds so that we may not be ruled by human reason but be rightly oriented and use logic as a servant. This is, indeed, the primary reason many struggle to receive the grace Jesus established and designed for us in the Lord's Supper. We have a fundamental problem with God using "stuff" from the material world to save. Yet in the person Jesus Himself is God's attachment to the physical to accomplish His salvific ends. The eternal Son of God, who has always existed, took on human flesh.

The human person Jesus is both fully God and fully man. Wholly and truly God and wholly and truly man. One person with two natures. God the eternal Son Himself took on a physical nature and forever will remain the God-man, both humanity and divinity in the person of the Christ, Jesus.

If God is okay binding Himself to the physical to save, then we should be okay with it too. We should be okay with Him using physical things in other manners to apply grace. If He wants to save, heal, or forgive using earthly means, we should recognize that as something God desires to do and has deemed right and good.

Imagine there was a blind man. Could Jesus cure His blindness simply by thinking it in His mind? Yes! But what if Jesus *wanted* to use means to restore the man's sight? Using something as earthly as spit, dirt, mud, and a washing in the water at the pool of Siloam (see John 9:6–7)? Is Jesus now less glorified for using means? Does He *not* get all the glory because He chose to use earthly elements to accomplish His ends? **Better yet, does this have to lead to idolatry and worship of spit, dirt, mud, and water? Not at all.**

The blind man did right to not question Jesus or call Him to task over His insistence upon using earthly means to do what otherwise could have been done by Him simply thinking it. The blind man did right to merely receive God's good gift by means. He trusted Jesus. Faith clings to the promise of God. He did not accuse the Lord of being ridiculous for suggesting such lowly things as a part of the healing. He did *not* get into an intellectual skirmish with the Christ over whether it was possible to cure blindness using such simple and meager means. He simply trusted Jesus' word.

So it is with the Sacraments. They are God's visible Word whereby He delivers His good gifts to us in a multiplicity of ways, all rooted in Jesus' earthly ministry (incarnation, sinless life, crucifixion, and resurrection). There's no competition or contradiction with faith alone. If God says, "Do this and receive sight," this is how you receive God's gifts. God uses earthly things to deliver, or hand over, the benefits of what Jesus accomplished on the cross.

These earthly things include the following:

- The death of the God-man on a real, physical, earthly tree
- The womb of a virgin woman to encapsulate the God of the universe
- Human preachers to preach His Word
- Human saliva, tongues, and vocal cords to do that preaching
- Physical sound waves that strike the eardrums of humans, who then believe the truth conveyed in physical traveling sound waves
- A physical book written by humans (though inspired by the Holy Spirit)
- Water to deliver life and cure spiritual blindness (Baptism)
- Bread and wine to "house" (in, with, and under) Himself to grant forgiveness (the Lord's Supper)
- A new earth that will join the new heaven

The Holy Spirit uses the aforementioned things to save.

The devil fights in abundance to block and rob faith.

God gives in abundance to create and preserve faith.

If you were under the immediate threat of death, would you do whatever our holy God asked of you to live? Picture yourself living amid an outbreak of fiery serpents that could end your life after only one bite.

Imagine God clearly communicated, in an unquestionable manner, the precise cure for this deadly plague. Yet the cure resonates with your personal sentiments as utterly absurd. It registers in your mind as illogical and far-fetched, superstitious even. Your emotional senses are triggered also because it makes you "feel weird" even considering it. Nonetheless, God said, "Do this and live."

The cure for this deadly epidemic is this:

Numbers 21:8:

> And the LORD said to Moses, "Make a fiery serpent
> and set it on a pole, and everyone who is bitten,
> when he sees it, shall live."

Would you, by faith alone, say "amen" and receive life, or resist on the grounds of "that's just weird"?

Okay, God, so with my two eyes, I simply look at a bronze serpent set on a pole and receive life? How? That makes no sense. Logic and reason functioning as master—and not servant—say that's impossible. That's weird. A bronze serpent set on a pole has no power. Why not just heal us by thinking it in Your mind? Why use means?

Nevertheless, Moses, by faith alone, said, "Amen."

Numbers 21:9:

> So Moses made a bronze serpent and set it on a
> pole. And if a serpent bit anyone, he would look at
> the bronze serpent and live.

So it is with the Sacraments (Baptism and the Lord's Supper). They are connected to God's Word whereby He delivers His good gifts to us. This is all rooted in Jesus' earthly ministry (incarnation, sinless life, crucifixion, and resurrection). There's no competition or contradiction with faith alone if God says, "Do this and live." If you are a Christian, this is how it takes place. God's promise to give you life is attached to earthly things to deliver the benefits of what Jesus accomplished on the cross for you. **He continues to use earthly elements (the Sacraments) attached to His triune name and promises to preserve our faith and to guard us against the world, flesh, and the devil. And ultimately, to see us safely home.**

May our faith cling to the promise of God like Moses and the Israelites who simply said "amen" to God's Word and received life.

Psalm 107:20:

> He sent out His word and healed them, and deliv-
> ered them from their destruction.

We hear God's Word. Through preaching.

We read God's Word. Through the Bible.

We eat God's Word. Through bread and wine. The Lord's Supper.

We bathe in God's Word. Through water. Baptism.

This is how God heals and delivers us.

There is no competition between Jesus and the Sacraments. We are not glorifying the Lord's Supper more than Jesus Himself. We have not placed bread and wine above the crucifixion. These are, perhaps, the innocent but misguided accusations of contemporary Christian thought. In contradiction, at the Lord's Table, Christ Himself accompanies us, binds us together with Him and with all saints (living and those present with Him), gives us immortality, and delivers the forgiveness of sin He earned for us on the cross.

We serve a God who gives in abundance. He blesses in a multiplicity of ways. In His kindness, He grants us tangible means that our faith clings to, tangible things such as bread and wine. He engages us as humans with five senses. He knows we doubt. He knows that our personal assessment of our own selves is limited. We fail to judge ourselves rightly in our sincerity and our level of commitment. We too often lean in on our degrees of spiritual growth. We constantly sin and are in need of forgiveness. He knows us and has considered our plight long before we have. He, therefore, shows up regularly, in many ways, with more grace. More forgiveness. More life. Because He is love. We do not only have our memory of our conversion experience (our testimony) to look to. We do not only have private prayers of confession of sin followed by absolution. We have the mystical union of Christ Himself in bread and wine. Each time we gather for Divine Service, we can gladly say, "Today, I was again granted forgiveness" based on Jesus' own words and His presence.

Matthew 26:26–28:

> Now as they were eating, Jesus took bread, and
> after blessing it broke it and gave it to the disci-
> ples, and said, "Take, eat; this is My body." And He
> took a cup, and when He had given thanks He gave
> it to them, saying, "Drink of it, all of you, for this is
> My blood of the covenant, which is poured out for
> many for the forgiveness of sins."

These realities lift us up from gazing so deeply within and bring us out of our heads. We can set our gaze on Jesus Himself and passively receive His gift of grace and forgiveness. Then, from a place of freedom, knowing we are secured and loved, we go out and bear fruit in keeping with repentance. The fruit that we bear is the result of repentance. It's what naturally follows those who experience the gift of repentance, which is contrition and faith.

Contrition is sorrow over sin. Faith then trusts God's words that we are forgiven. Judas took his own life because he did not trust in God's promise of forgiveness. He trusted in his own inner word of despair and guilt, making himself the jury and judge and demanding self-punishment, which ended in suicide.

Peter, on the other hand, after his denial of Jesus three times, did not take his own life out of despair. I can imagine he was deeply discouraged and disappointed in himself. We all can relate to that, right? He experienced repentance, which, again, is contrition and faith—that is, sorrow over sin and trust in God's promise of forgiveness. Therefore, rather than taking his own life, he received life from his Lord and went on bearing good fruit. Or to say it another way, he went on doing good works in the world for the sake of those around him (neighbors). He did all this empowered by God's Word and Sacraments.

HISTORICAL PERSPECTIVE (THAT LONG)

These realities concerning the Sacraments are not new and novel ideas. In fact, they are the teachings the universal Church has held to the longest. The opening line to my song titled "That Long" from my EP *Christ for You* says:

Do you know how long it had been,
without any significant disagreement,
that Christ was bodily present in the bread
and the wine?
Better watch these new doctrines!
You know how long it took for someone to start teaching
"is" means "represents"? Naw, you can't ignore thus,
bruh.

The hook enters and takes over the song. If you know the song, feel free to rap along with the lyrics. Out loud or in your head if you're around people:

One five zero zero, that long!
One five zero zero, that long!
One five zero zero, facts,
Boy, I'm talking about the first fifteen hundred.
One five zero zero, that long!
One five zero zero, that long!

One five zero zero, facts.
Boy, I'm talking about the first fifteen hundred.

I recall first finding this out. My jaw dropped! I was utterly shocked that in all my years as a believer I had never heard this claim. Not as a youth or as a teen coming up in church. In all my formal theological training in Reformed Baptist institutions, I was never confronted with it. Not once. I confess I felt something akin to betrayal. Not deeply, but a mild level of disappointment. It resonated like someone was trying to keep something away from me.

I regretted not even being presented with the option to think it through on my own or at least in a communal context in the institution. This would have provided a space for students and the trained scholars to engage together on teachings that our dear brothers and sisters who went before us believed deeply, wrote about, and gave their lives for. It would have been an excellent time of learning and engagement in the controlled academic environment, in my opinion.

Nevertheless, during my time at Concordia Seminary in St. Louis, I delightfully gained that experience. That kind of digging is still fueling my fire to the present moment and I suspect will continue to until Jesus returns. In the second verse of the song "That Long," I address the historicity of it all and the consensus the Early Church Fathers maintained. Are you ready to rap along again? Let's go! It says this:

We can't ignore Ethiopia
these Africans never been colonized.
Trace them back to the Book of Acts

to the eunuch that asked to be baptized.
They never came under the papacy,
gave the cup and the bread to the laity.
And when Luther met Michael the deacon
they're both in agreement that Jesus in bread and wine
(bodily).
Really ain't no way to debate this
even dating back to Ignatius
he was born in AD 35
and discipled by the apostle John
he taught the body in bread
and the African known as Augustine
can't forget about Irenaeus
and the Martyr known as Justin.
From Cyril to Thomas Aquinas
the testimony of the ancient
Church is really universal
until Zwingli decided to change it
and Calvin started placing his limits (in his Institutes)
on Jesus' metaphysics
and lead with his presuppositions
and keeping them over the Scriptures, facts.

It should be noted that the majority of Christians that have ever existed and that exist today hold to Jesus being bodily present in the bread and wine. Though there may be nuances in the way different groups get at it, the confession is nearly the same. This means that the most novel and contemporary view of the Lord's Supper is held by the smallest number of Christians. Nor has their novel idea been around that long. **Obviously, the fact that the majority of people believe in a thing does not make it right. History testifies to that.** Yet, this consensus is curious because the symbolic view is relatively foreign to Church history. That's for certain a bad sign and should be noted.

Some will say that this is simply a holdover from Rome, garbage that Luther forgot to take out from when the Roman Catholics were over his house. That is why I made this statement:

> **We can't ignore Ethiopia, these Africans never been colonized. Trace them back to the Book of Acts to the eunuch that asked to be baptized. They never came under the papacy, gave the cup and the bread to the laity. And when Luther met Michael the deacon, they're both in agreement that Jesus in bread and wine (bodily).**

The Ethiopian Church did not submit to the Roman Catholic Church. They had a Bible written in their own language before Luther's translation of the Bible into German. And they, unlike the Roman Catholic Church, gave the cup and the bread to parishioners. This is a strong argument to chisel away at the misperception that Luther had held on to an idea that originated with Rome. The Ethiopian Church and its practices prove that wrong.

Let me not fail to mention that those Early Church Fathers I mentioned in the verse above taught these truths before the Roman Catholic Church developed into what it was during Luther's day and ours. Also, one should consider that the mystical union of the Lord's Supper was held by Eastern Church Fathers as well. So the notion that Rome invented the Eucharist doctrine and that Luther simply wouldn't let go of it is debunked with mounds of evidence dating back to 1500 and counting.

In addition, I also learned that my dear brother Luther and a host of other scholars with him entered the theological boxing ring to hash these matters out. Although there was some agreement reached on other theological matters, they ultimately could not agree on the nature of the Lord's Supper. Luther was committed to Jesus' words and refused to be swayed. Now let's read the lyrics from the first verse. They go as follows:

Take them to the Marburg Colloquy.
Luther versus Zwingli it's 'bout to be
two prominent scholars from 1529
I promise they're boxing theology.
"This is My body," he carved.
Luther wrote that in some chalk
then covered it with a cloth
but patiently waited to show it.
Shout out to Philip of Hesse he
wrote letters to set up successfully
this meeting between these legendary figures
he figured his efforts would definitely
form a political front
so Charles the V does not get what he wants
to stick with the script of the edict of Worms
to basically seek out and delete the Reformers.

But Luther wrote, "This is My body,"
emphasis on the word "is."
This is God's promise
when He spoke the Words of Institution.
Homeboy "is" means "is"
it is Christ's body.
Zwingli ain't like it
because it contradicted rationalism
now he's trying to explain it
instead of sticking with the plain meaning
of what the boy's reading
he elevated reason and he changed it, facts.

This brief summary of the event at the Marburg Colloquy in 1529 sets the historical scene of when things shifted. It can be argued that this defining moment is the reason some in contemporary Christianity hold a symbolic view of the Lord's Supper, unfortunately. Many assume they see symbolism in the Scriptures objectively. However, most are unaware that this interpretive decision was made for them about five hundred years ago. Had we lived before this meeting in 1529, we would most likely have never questioned the reality that Jesus is bodily present in the elements.

Yet because everyone reading this book or hearing it read was born after this event in 1529, some believe Jesus was being metaphorical when He instituted the Lord's Supper. This has much to do with the cultural shift happening in 1529. Society as a whole was beginning to move away from the supernatural ways of seeing the world to more of a scientific way of viewing the world. The idea was budding that what we know must be derived from hard-core testable evidence as opposed to ancient spooky ideas of gods, demons, and the supernatural.

The fuller expression of this sentiment and ideology is known as the Enlightenment. Most understand it as digging its roots in the ground during the seventeenth and eighteenth centuries, but the early stages of those ideas were percolating during Luther's day—which posed a threat to biblical interpretation. The temptation was to alter things that appeared too weird. How can Jesus be bodily present in mere bread and wine? Some thought that was just not rational. This was a new challenge to the way the oldest of saints understood Jesus' own words. There were those who were taught directly by the apostle John himself that Jesus' bodily presence was in the earthly elements. John taught people such as Ignatius and arguably Polycarp. We have writings from them confessing that the true body and blood of Jesus are mysteriously present with the communion meal. We also have writings from the next generation of students. **This means that the apostles taught the same idea concerning the Lord's Table.** And one and two generations removed from Jesus Himself were taught it and preached it to others. This is certainly compelling evidence that must be considered and should not be easily dismissed.

With this in mind, we should take seriously that Jesus made this claim toward the end of His life and pending crucifixion. The stakes were high. He chose His words carefully and intentionally. He said, while holding bread, "This is My body." And while holding wine, He said, "This is My blood." Those are His words.

Is means "is," even if used in a metaphor, a parable, or plain and literal speech.

If a guy were to say, "My girl is represented by this flower," then that would make little sense and fail to communicate his intended compliment. It could call to mind characteristics and aspects that confuse what he's trying to say. How does the flower represent his girlfriend? Is she dirty? Should she expect not to live long? Does she shrivel and smell bad eventually? You get the point. So it is if Jesus' words were "My body is represented by this bread" or "My blood is represented by this wine." That only confuses things.

This it's why it's crucial to stick with the inspired Word in the Scriptures. The word is not *represents* but *is*. There's no metaphor in the statement at all. The text also does not record a confusion on the part of the disciples at the table with Him in the Upper Room that day. The text does not note any follow-up questions for clarity, nor does it raise accusations of the absurdity concerning this mystery. Jesus is the Word Himself (John 1:1). It's safe to say that Jesus knows how to express Himself clearly during these final and important moments. He meant what He said: *is*.

GNOSTICISM

Another philosophical idea that threatened the true exposition of Jesus' own words is Gnosticism. In summary, Gnosticism is a false teaching that started to show up in its infant stages during the New Testament era. Among many other interesting and obscure ideologies, Gnosticism taught that matter, or material, is evil. The physical is bad and the spirit is good. They championed secret supreme knowledge that only a few had access to as the way of salvation.

For these reasons, their subscribers denied biblical Christianity's validity. They particularly dismissed the notion that God came in the flesh. They could not fathom the thought that a holy God would unite Himself to an evil, material human body. Again, for them, the physical world was bad. This is why John the beloved argued against any who would deny that Jesus came in the flesh. First John 4:1–3 reads:

> Beloved, do not believe every spirit, but test the spirits to see whether they are from God, for many false prophets have gone out into the world. By this you know the Spirit of God: every spirit that confesses that Jesus Christ has come in the flesh is from God, and every spirit that does not confess Jesus is not from God. This is the spirit of the anti-christ, which you heard was coming and now is in the world already.

Unfortunately, the influence of this ancient heresy is ever present, alive and well. It still camps out near the Christians, seeking to inject its poison into the Christian bloodstream. Contemporary Christians become functional Gnostics when they turn their nose up at the very thought that God would use physical bread and wine or water to deliver Christ and His gifts. It is believed that true spirituality must be invisible and ethereal.

It seems cheap, barbaric, and unsophisticated of God to stoop so low as to use such meager earthly things. Many believe these ideas are holdovers from the undeveloped ancient world and that we have arrived at a stage of enlightenment and no longer need to entertain such outdated and old-school ways of thinking about the Lord's Supper.

People troll the "crazy" Christians who literally take God at His Word. They think it's an insult to say, "You crazy people take the Bible and Jesus' words about the Lord's Supper literally?" Actually, I'm okay with that insult. "FLAME takes Jesus' words literally! He's crazy." **Yeah, I'm okay with that. Put that on my tombstone: "FLAME took Jesus' words literally."** Wherever the Gnostics are today, they are probably on their feet giving a standing ovation to the Christians who have embraced their heretical concept of the physical and material world being off-limits for God's use in His good plan of redemption.

What people tend to forget is that God regularly uses the material world to accomplish His saving will. The Second Person of the Trinity, the Son of God, took on human flesh. The Bible was written by humans. God uses our prayers, which come from our physical bodies. Even if you pray "in your head," that's still physical material at work dispensing those thoughts up to God. He uses us to help one another as tools in His hands. In that way, we become His hands and feet, physical beings. The list goes on, culminating in the new heaven and the new earth. God has deemed His creation good, not evil. He delights in using it as a part of His redemptive plan.

TRANSUBSTANTIATION VERSUS CONSUBSTANTIATION

It should also be noted that Lutherans aim to argue only what the Bible reveals. We do not seek to fully grasp what cannot be fully grasped by depending on philosophy. Nor are we willing to be restricted by the rules of philosophy to describe what God has left to mystery. For that reason, it should be noted that we do not hold to either transubstantiation or consubstantiation. These are well-intended efforts to describe the holy mystery of the Eucharist but ones that are not Lutheran.

In short, transubstantiation is the position of the Roman Catholic Church. It teaches that Jesus is bodily present in the Eucharist but that the elements of bread and wine only appear to be bread and wine. They'd say that the elements transubstantiated—that the substance of the bread and wine are changed to Jesus' actual body and blood. Lutherans would agree that Jesus is bodily present in the elements, but we differ in that, based on both Jesus' and Paul's words, we profess that the bread is still actual bread and the wine remains actual wine.

Consubstantiation is the attempt to describe what people think Lutherans believe. We do not hold to consubstantiation, nor has it been a term used in Lutheran history. It is the notion that the elements of bread and wine joined with Jesus' body and blood, taking on a new, joined nature. This is another attempt to use philosophy to describe a mysterious occurrence. For this reason, Luther and the Lutheran tradition have not attempted to describe the miraculous nature of the Eucharist.

A collection of prepositions were used by Luther to simply say that we only confess what Jesus said—that He is present. Nothing more. Nothing less. Therefore, you'll hear Lutherans say that Jesus is "in, with, and under" the bread and wine. Other terms such as "real presence" or the "mystical union" have been used to keep it simple and to allow only room for what is revealed without a deep philosophical dive into trying to explain it all. Typically, if the term "real presence" is used, Lutherans will rightly add that it's possible to use that term and not mean what Lutherans mean when they use it.

Some Calvinists are okay talking about a "real presence." Yet they may mean that Jesus is "spiritually present" by His spiritual nature and that the Holy Spirit lets His children somehow be drawn upward to the Lord during Communion. The Bible teaches that nowhere, respectfully. So when they use the term "real presence," we would reject their use and meaning. For reasons like these, Lutherans aim to keep it simple and limited to what's clearly said in the Bible. That in, with, and under real bread is His body, and in, with, and under actual wine is His blood. How? He did not say nor explain. He just stated the truth and what He wanted to reveal to His disciples, which extends to us.

NOT ONE BONE WILL BE BROKEN

Many who hold to a symbolic view, like I once did, most likely haven't considered a few other things. Another song of mine from the *Christ for You* EP titled "Upper Room" raises some interesting points to consider. The verse goes as follows:

> *Let me show you this*
> *have you noticed this.*
> *Matthew 26:26 never says*
> *that the body of Jesus was broken like bread.*
> *That's the complete opposite of what the prophecy says.*
> *Not one bone in His body will be broken*
> *so how the bread broken represent the body then.*

You say the wine represents the blood because it's red
but the bread color doesn't represent the body.
Ain't that arbitrary how we made it symbolic
then what does eating bread and drinking wine say
about his atonement if it only represents the body
but the body wasn't broken.
That's the problem.

It is stated in a few places throughout the Old Testament that the Messiah will not experience a broken bone. For example, Psalm 34:20 states it this way:

> He keeps all His bones; not one of them is broken.

The Gospel of John recalls this prophecy and illustrates that it was fulfilled in Christ. John 19:33–36 says:

> But when they came to Jesus and saw that He was already dead, they did not break His legs. But one of the soldiers pierced His side with a spear, and at once there came out blood and water. He who saw it has borne witness—his testimony is true, and he knows that he is telling the truth—that you also may believe. For these things took place that the Scripture might be fulfilled: "Not one of His bones will be broken."

With this being the case, it's important to highlight that the bread Jesus broke in the Upper Room as He was establishing the Lord's Supper was not representative of His body being broken. This is clear based on the prophecy of Scripture that His body would not be broken. Not one bone. Here is where the reaching starts. People start saying things like "His emotional spirit was broken" or "His flesh was beaten, which broke some skin." Those are merely efforts to be consistent with the symbolic view of the Supper. The Bible does not describe those things as a "breaking of Jesus." To assume so is going beyond what's revealed in the Bible. That's the wrong thing to do.

The bread was broken so that Jesus could distribute it to His disciples. The type of bread that they partook of needed to be pulled apart and passed around. Therefore, it's described as being broken. Jesus was not saying they were about to break His body as represented by His treatment of the bread. That is reading into the text what is not there. That's the wrong thing to do.

Furthermore, it is rather arbitrary to say that Jesus chose wine because it's red like blood. In that case, it should be pointed out that no one teaches that Jesus chose bread because it matched the color of His human flesh. Why do some use that line of thinking for the wine but not the bread? Curious. The point here is not to be nitpicky or trivial but to highlight the lengths some go to, simply in an effort to not seem strange to skeptics or to distance ourselves from all things affiliated with Roman Catholics.

The simple answer is that Jesus chose bread and wine because He wanted to. He can do that. Those from the Reformed Baptist circle (and Reformed in general) should be particularly alarmed by the metaphoric view since they hold to *sola scriptura*, which is a Latin phrase that means "Scripture alone." Sola scriptura is a principle birthed out of Luther's Reformation. Its primary aim is to establish that the Scriptures are sufficient, supreme, and our final authority concerning matters of spiritual life. Therefore, all things that pertain to salvation and the Christian journey can be found implicitly or explicitly in the Bible.

With that being confessed from the Reformed, of which I used to be, I could not allow myself to interpret Jesus' word *is* to mean "represent." Lutherans and most orthodox Christians believe that the Bible was inspired by the Holy Spirit. Although He used humans to write it, He nonetheless led, influenced, and oversaw the entire process, all the way down to what words He wanted used. Yes, He used people's natural skill sets, educations, aptitudes, and cultural influences based on the context of their environment. Yet the Holy Spirit was fully involved in having said all that He wanted said consistent with the triune counsel.

Let me draw your attention to another important factor for consideration. As I began to process the parallels between the Lord's Supper being established in the Upper Room on the day the Jews were celebrating Passover, I was floored. Scripture clearly confesses that Jesus is the Passover Lamb who came to take away the sins of the world (see John 1:29). **It was important to Jesus to institute the Lord's Supper on the exact day both He and His disciples met.**

The hook (chorus) on my song "Passover Lamb" from *Christ for You* says:

Jesus is the Great I Am.
See the parallels
Jesus the Passover Lamb.
Did they eat the lamb
Yes, yes, they ate the lamb (literally).

Did they eat the lamb
Yes, yes, they ate the lamb, for real.

In the old covenant, as a celebration and commemoration of the day the Lord delivered His people from Pharaoh and allowed death to pass over the homes of His children, they would sacrifice a lamb and eat the lamb that was sacrificed. Jesus makes the announcement that He is the Lamb of God and then tells His disciples that the bread they are about to eat is His body. The wine they are about to drink is His blood. Just like the people of God literally ate the sacrificed lamb, so do we partake of the body and blood of the ultimate sacrificial Lamb: Christ Jesus, our Lord.

This parallel is astounding.

The second verse of that same song makes mention of a final point I'd like to share. The verse reads:

Jesus said I am the vine.
Jesus said I am the door (T-H-E).
Interpret this the way you want to do it
got the Scriptures saying Jesus represents the door.
But that don't make sense does it.
Jesus is the vine.
He is the life source
and the way to get to God.
Plus He said "the" vine
not "a" vine
some random vine
some random door

better be careful making metaphors.
Plus He said "I Am" the way
the truth the life (the Light)
resurrection and the life
"I Am" the bread of life.
Want to make the "I Am" statements the symbolic type
like "I Am" that "I Am"
that's denying Christ.
Yes He used some symbolism here to make His point
don't miss His point
to the truths though to which they point.
These passages are not parallel with the other
He's not holding objects up like the Lord's Supper.

The move people typically make to argue that Jesus' words are metaphorical is that they skip to the "I Am" statements. Although the "I Am" statements of Jesus do not parallel the Lord's Supper passage, people try to force a connection. Jesus says He is the door and that He is the vine. These are both true statements. Jesus is the door to heaven. He is the vine through which we must be connected to draw eternal life and sustenance. Though He used images to make His point, they are still true statements about Him. You cannot inherit eternal life without coming by way of Him or without being connected to Him.

In addition, John continues to list more "I Am" statements concerning Jesus. Jesus says, "I am" the door, "I am" the vine, "I am" the way, the truth, and the life, "I am" the light of the world, and finally culminating with the absolute statement "I AM" (John

8:58; see also John 8:24, 28). These are all one consistent statement. One confession of His "I Am"-ness, if you will. You cannot break them up. Jesus is all these things.

When Jesus says He is the vine or the door, Jesus is also claiming to be the great "I AM" based on the grammar and flow of thought. You can't make one or two of the "I Am" statements symbolic and then claim that the rest are literal. The grammar doesn't allow it, nor is that true of Jesus' existence. Also, He was not holding up objects like He was in the Upper Room with the bread and the wine.

In John 14–15, He says "I am *the* vine"—*the*—not "a" vine, like some random vine. He says "I am *the* door"—*the*—not "a" door, like some random door. While instituting the Lord's Supper, He was not using symbolism or making a metaphor. He was actually holding the elements in His hands, saying, "These right here, these things that are in My hands right now that you all can see with your eyes and touch with your hands and taste with your tongues, are My body and blood." That is why the "I Am" statements should not be confused with the Lord's Supper. They are different types of grammatical texts communicating different truths about Jesus.

When Jesus said hard things to His followers in John 6, they thought He was insane, and many departed from Him.

John 6:52–53 says:

> The Jews then disputed among themselves, saying,
> "How can this man give us His flesh to eat?" So
> Jesus said to them, "Truly, truly, I say to you,
> unless you eat the flesh of the Son of Man and
> drink His blood, you have no life in you."

It goes on to say in verses 60–61:

> When many of His disciples heard it, they said,
> "This is a hard saying; who can listen to it?" But
> Jesus, knowing in Himself that His disciples were
> grumbling about this, said to them, "Do you take
> offense at this?"

This resulted in two different confessions and reactions. Verses 66–68 read:

> After this many of His disciples turned back and
> no longer walked with Him. So Jesus said to the
> twelve, "Do you want to go away as well?" Simon
> Peter answered Him, "Lord, to whom shall we go?
> You have the words of eternal life."

Notice Jesus never turned to His critics to lighten the load. He never attempted to break the awkward silence of His hard statement. Not once did He soften His words to make them more palatable to the rational mind. The Bible does not record Him saying, "Okay, okay, I wasn't saying literally eat My flesh and drink My blood. That'd be crazy, right? I was saying metaphorically." No, He let His words sit in their full weight. He even let people walk away. He didn't chase them down so He could be more seeker-friendly and likable. He stood on His words because He meant them.

It should be noted that Jesus was not promoting cannibalism either. That would have been a sin against the Law to eat human flesh. Nor was He saying to eat His body as it was or drink His blood as it was. He was speaking about His mysterious bodily presence in the bread and wine. In this meal, He promises us the forgiveness of sin, to unite us with Himself, and to make us one with the entire family of Christ.

As I worked through these things, I began to hear God's voice in a fresh new way, all rooted in the Scriptures. My already existing ideas of being justified by faith alone were expanded and set back into proper position. Like a diamond that needs to be readjusted and placed back into its claw collet, that position is right alongside the Sacraments.

The Sacraments were never intended to be separated from the confession of justification by faith. The tradition I came from drove a wedge between this happily married couple. Yet God saw fit to expose me to their partnership—of which I was never made aware. From then on, I began to understand how they were meant to be together, and I had to tell the world about this wonderful dynamic that God established to deliver His salvific gifts to us. For our forgiveness. For our comfort. For our assurance.

Before then, I was in a similar place as many: despair. The year 2020 was hard for many reasons: social ills, pestilence, personal loss. The list goes on. That year, I witnessed many leave the Christian faith and others who were gravely close to doing so. I wanted them to hear Christianity represented in a way that perhaps they never had before, to reimagine their Lord in a more biblical way that highlights His true essence and character.

I wrote these lyrics to speak to them about the treasure God revealed to me. One that was hidden in the confessional Lutheran tradition. A treasure He preserved there for the weary traveler. They read:

[Verse 1]
Lil Brody say he hurt he popped an extra dose.
Disillusioned by the church he say he hecka ghost
He say the Western Church
tasting hecka gross.
I say before you go check that Extra Nos.
You search and you search and you're searching for
something that's more than a metaphor
something that you can experience
that's deeper than what you've been hearing it's
a supper that He instituted
along the way it got polluted
but when the Church was persecuted
they clung to it and ain't lose it.
They found their identity not in ethnicity
but in something that was rooted
in the promise that He made to them
in the elements He gave to them
and He said that He would save through them
give us life and forgave through them
make us one with God the Son
with bread and wine as the conduit.
[Hook]
I know you by name, yes I do.
When I'm coming down, it's for you.
As I come around, it's for you.
Lord's Supper bread and wine, it's for you.
I know you by name, yes I do.

When I'm coming down, it's for you.
As I come around, it's for you.
Lord's Supper bread and wine, it's for you.
[Verse 2]
What you're looking for yeah it's outside of us.
They say how you keep the faith
I say He promised us
immortality is ours it's applied to us
every time we eat His flesh and drink His blood.
Go look it up look it up look it up.
God so good He had to hook it up
because the conscience gets shook'n up
now we're doing work trying to cook it up.
Yeah Jesus He gave us a pledge
because He knew we'd get stuck in our heads
so He gave us a seal that's filled with a mystery
He in the midst of the bread.
Under in and with the bread.
Under in and with the wine.
(Bodily? Wow!)
Now this universal promise He brings it down
then I make it mine.
So when we struggle with doubt
we do not look to our fruit or our purity.
That will not bring security.
It's the supper He instituted that'll cure me.
[Hook]

This is one of my favorite songs I've written. I can just close my eyes and contemplate the sweetness of God delivering His Word to us through the Holy Meal. Indeed, Christ Himself for us. For our joy. For our peace. The power is in God's Word. Yes, it's real bread. Yes, it's real wine. Nevertheless, faith clings to the promise, and He will meet us as often as we participate in the Eucharist. He says as often as we do this, we do it in remembrance of Him (1 Corinthians 11:25).

People hear the words "in remembrance of Me" and again think this proves a symbolic and metaphorical understanding of Communion. That interpretation is unnecessary and untrue. We do this all the time. I heard it put this way: whenever we celebrate a person's birthday party, we do it in remembrance of their birthday. Yet they do not need to be absent. They can still be physically present while we gather to do something in memory of them. This is a perfectly fitting parallel that demonstrates the same reality taking place at the Lord's Table. Yes, we are remembering Jesus, His words, and what He accomplished and is continuing to accomplish for us. Daily and every second of every moment. All while He is present at the Table with us to feed us life and sustenance through His own body and blood. Present in, with, and under the elements. What a sweet mystery. Grace on grace on grace. May the Lord soften hard hearts who resist this truth so that they come to know of the multiplicity of ways God blesses us and delivers His gifts. May He renew those of us who are accustomed to this reality and guard us from growing numb to it and the temptation to simply see it as an external ritual with hearts detached. By the power of His Holy Spirit who indwells the Church. Amen.

LOSING SALVATION?

After hearing of these wonderful truths, a person brought up the fact that Lutherans believe that someone can walk away from their faith (historically called apostasy). He asked, "So does the Holy Spirit leave the indwelled presence of the believer when they denounce Christ? I thought Ephesians 4 says we are sealed until the day of redemption." To which I responded: "Thanks for asking, bro bro."

Before I get into the rest of my response, I want to say this: we must remember to interpret the Scriptures in view of the whole of Scripture. To isolate a verse away from the immediate context and the broader context of Scripture gets us into trouble.

Calvinists have done a great job with collecting the Scriptures related to God keeping us (amen!) but have not done the same quality job with the warning passages. They reduce them down to being hypothetical, or they dismiss them as proof that a person was "never with us in the first place." That's not good sola scriptura. It is, however, logically consistent with the five-point TULIP.

But back to the question at hand.

1. That seal in Ephesians is speaking to the marking or branding God places on us, namely the Holy Spirit. He labels us as His. The image is of a wax seal on a scroll, or the branding on a bondservant. Praise God, by His Spirit, He marks us by giving us the Holy Spirit. Also, He marks us through Baptism and the Lord's Supper. There, too, He "tattoos" us as His own. This is a beautiful reality. We can find much assurance and comfort here.

2. Yet the Bible does not only confess Ephesians 1:13 or Ephesians 4:30. Paul says elsewhere, in 1 Timothy 1:18–20:

> Wage the good warfare, holding faith and a
> good conscience. By rejecting this, some have
> made shipwreck of their faith, among whom
> are Hymenaeus and Alexander, whom I have
> handed over to Satan that they may learn not to
> blaspheme.

The plain reading of this text—without the mental gymnastics that are a temptation among my Calvinist friends—confesses that some have made shipwreck of *their* faith, meaning they had genuine faith.

It does *not* say they made shipwreck of a faith they never really had or thought they had but was never theirs in the first place. That's called eisegesis, or reading into the text. That's the *wrong* thing to do.

Also, the difficult and weighty text Hebrews 6:4–6:

> For it is impossible, in the case of those who have
> once been enlightened, who have tasted the heav-
> enly gift, and have shared in the Holy Spirit, and
> have tasted the goodness of the word of God and
> the powers of the age to come, and then have
> fallen away, to restore them again to repentance.

First, a good and honest Calvinist knows that this description can*not* define a nonbeliever or simply the Old Testament people of God, because the things described are *only* brought on by regeneration and new birth: "once been enlightened, who have tasted the heavenly gift, and have shared in the Holy Spirit, and have tasted the goodness of the word of God and the powers of the age to come." Again, this does *not* sound like a description of someone outside the faith.

Also, this difficult passage rightly points out that a person who once had "been enlightened" (regeneration/eyes opened by the Spirit) can be so done with God and His ways that their hardness of heart will *not* allow them to repent—that repentance, therefore, apparently becomes off limits for them. Selah. Yet, a person with a troubled conscience should still turn to God's promises.

3.   Having said all that, God has graciously provided means for us to endure to the end. It is the Calvinist system that is preoccupied with "am I in or out?" because of false teachings like double predestination and limited atonement, respectfully.

Lutherans don't live in this headspace. Why? Because we are looking outside of us, extra nos. We are looking to God's promises in the objective work on the cross for all. We are looking to the Sacraments, the visible Word of God, where God promises to meet us with forgiveness and immortality. We have Confession and Absolution. And election. We have God's promise that He will forgive our sin. In fact, Jesus taught us to pray that way: "Give us this day our daily bread; and forgive us our trespasses." He taught us to pray that way, and He will honor our prayers for forgiveness.

Again, Lutherans don't have to live in this headspace. Why? We are busy serving our neighbor and not in our heads so much. When we sin and the Law kills us, we repent (which is contrition and faith). God gives us the faith to believe we are forgiven. That's the Gospel. Then we "bear fruit in keeping with repentance" (Matthew 3:8). That fruit is the result of repentance. With it, we serve those around us. That's the cycle until Jesus returns.

This is why we boast in the Lord, to use Paul's words, about our assurance. We can take the warning passages seriously, and we can rest in God's promises, knowing that Jesus died for sinners like us.

So we confess that, yes, there is a tension in Scripture. We don't like it as much as anyone. Yet we do not seek to speak where the Bible is silent nor to close the gap God has left open. John Calvin himself sought to reconcile this tension in the Bible by connecting dots, wrongfully. We should let the tension exist and humbly bow our knee to what is revealed, although it is not intellectually satisfying. Much more can be said. I digress.

Clearly, the person who asked me was from the Reformed camp. My aim was to lift him out of the mindset that is almost obsessively concerned with the loss of salvation. I remember that being ever present in my thinking. If I'm honest, I to this day still have to guard against it. Once you've been drenched in a style of thinking for eighteen years, it doesn't just go away. **As I've been in the Lutheran space for over two years now, it's interesting to observe that this dark cloud of fear and anxiety does not follow the average parishioner.**

I'm not romanticizing Lutheranism as if it's perfect and has nothing to guard against. Yet when I consider the headspace that I know persists all too often for many in the Reformed camp, I just don't witness that same terror and fright among other traditions, particularly confessional Lutheranism. The fright of "am I in or out? Am I elect or am I deceived?"

I love the way Gene Veith Jr. put it in his book *The Spirituality of the Cross*. He says,

> Thus, Lutheran spirituality, properly speaking, is not some static state of bliss, but a dynamic oscillation between lows and highs, knowledge of sin and knowledge of forgiveness, repentance, and assurance. The Gospel is to predominate, however, in the words of C. F. W. Walther, so that the Lutheran Christian lives in a state of grace.[7]

I could not agree more.

At times, it felt like the opposite in my former tradition, that many dwelled in a perpetual state of "grace-fear," both resting and frightened at the same time. It's like being asleep but not in a deep sleep, so much so that when you wake up you still feel sleepy from not getting good sleep while you were sleeping.

Perhaps it has to do with an inaccurate notion of "falling away" from your faith. The connotation is that it somehow happens unbeknownst to you. As if you look up one day and realize, "Oh wait, I fell away." Or an inaccurate notion of "losing your faith," as if, unbeknownst to you, you misplace your faith like a pair of lost keys and just can't seem to find it anywhere.

What I observe from Scripture is that those who part ways with God consciously choose to. They decided to live a lifestyle contrary to the Christian way, or they mindfully chose to denounce belief in the God of Scripture. Even false prophets appear to be spoken of as

---

7   Gene Edward Veith Jr., *The Spirituality of the Cross*, revised edition (St. Louis: Concordia Publishing House, 2010), 38.

being cognitively aware that they are deceiving others for personal gain. The Bible doesn't position apostasy as a thing that catches you off guard and surprises you in the end. It might start subtly and worsen, but those who believe in Jesus do not all of a sudden just stop believing in Him out of nowhere.

My assessment is that this is the result of teaching justification by faith alone, detached from the "whole counsel of God," to use Paul's words. Justification by faith coupled with double predestination and limited atonement creates an internal conflict, particularly for those who are thinking about their faith. Particularly for those who are consciously working through their theology and following it to its logical end.

When justification by faith alone is divorced from the other Means of Grace (the visible Word of God, the Sacraments), then preaching can become a point of conflict. How so, you ask? As the Word of God is being preached, both Law and Gospel, we are more prone to lock in on the Law and thus set out to prove our salvation. We try to muster up enough strength to be good people and really, really, really love God with all our heart's affections.

These activities become good things gone wrong. They morph into efforts to prove that we are really saved and love God more than anything. The focus becomes Godward obedience to the Law, motivated by anxiety to earn our way in, or at least to continually secure our seat in heaven. After all, you don't want to lose your seat because the moment you move, it might get taken away. If you notice, that direction of the moral uprightness and internal monitoring is set vertically. Progressive sanctification becomes one's obsession.

One must get better and better and better, showing God how genuine they are toward Him, how deeply they despise the world and the things in it because all they want is Him. This typically turns into a fighting match with the material world and the many good things in it. You start hearing well-intended but extreme exaggerated sentiments like "Jesus over career" or "I only live for God." People begin to pit good things against God. They say things like "God is enough. I don't need cars, money, education, clothes, shoes, family—just give me Jesus! As long as I have Him, I'm good!"

It's not that the resolve to be fully content in God alone is wrong. Please don't hear me saying that. God designed us to live in His good creation with one another. He desires to give us resources to serve one another. He is not expecting us to vehemently despise the many "worldly" (not immoral) elements on earth. He gave us family. He gave us minds to attain knowledge of the known world. He gave us creativity to invent cars, fashion, and technology, and to monetize them into careers. These are His good ideas for us. We should enjoy them and fully embrace them. We should cherish creation and spend time in the great outdoors, exploring and being awestruck by His intricate detail in our vast universe. We should love scientific discovery and see His hand at work.

He gave us all these things to enjoy and to care for one another with. He doesn't want us to keep our distance from the world so as to avoid being tainted. No, He wants us to responsibly engage the world around us, to interact with people from diverse backgrounds, worldviews, and experiences, to share things in common with them, to seek their good, and to cultivate an environment they can flourish in.

He doesn't delight in seeing His children isolated and detached from the world, in the house 24/7, in the dark, in hopes to avoid getting dirty. How can we share with others the gifts and talents He placed in us? How will others benefit from the unique personality God gave us to bless others with? Our curiosities? Our humor? Our intelligence? How can we receive from others what they possess from God for our benefit? This is evident when we go visit the doctor or go to the grocery store to pick up food that the farmers skillfully produced for us. In those moments, it's more clearly seen that we benefit from other people's skill sets and vocations.

These horizontal emphases are downplayed when you pit God against the world and forcibly position people's lives vertically in an exaggerated way, upward toward singularly hating sin more and more, progressively growing in your affections for God, and avoiding interaction with people and things so as to remain secure from temptation.

Unfortunately, preaching is heard by the people across the pulpit in these ways when the Christian life isn't framed properly. People are forced to lean deeply into their own performance as proof that they are saved and serious about God

- when parishioners don't understand the two types of righteousness (first passively receiving from God and then actively lived out before one another);

- when they don't know the Law/Gospel distinction (how God's Word is doing two things: crushing us or bringing us life);

- when they don't hear about the functional uses of the Law (a curb from sin, a mirror, a guide);

- when they don't know the varying ways God delivers His grace (the preached Word, the written Word, and the visible Word: the Sacraments, the Lord's Supper and Baptism); and

- when people don't have a safe place and a church culture that has normalized the confession of sin followed by the sweet, life-giving Words of Absolution.

These biblical realities expressed in categories and language codified in the Lutheran tradition help rightly orient us as people experiencing the vast complexities included in the human experience—in particular, the human Christian experience. In the aforementioned categories, one will find an acute grasp of the paradoxical and perplexing nature of Christian human affairs. One will notice the relevance of the Bible as a book that "gets us," a book inspired by God the Holy Spirit, who knows human nature and the full range of what people are like and the world they inhabit.

Lutheranism has provided me the spectrum to be my full self. My complex, diverse, curious, and confusing self. I can live in the world and enjoy its many delights and pleasures. I can explore the vast diversity of what life has to offer within the boundaries and parameters God put in place for our good. I can trust that the Holy Spirit, through the communication of His Word as Law, will course-correct me if I start to drift or veer. I don't have to sink into the despair of perfectionism because the Holy Spirit will use His

Word's function as Gospel to vivify me, to bring me life afresh and renew my spirit through forgiveness and assurance.

I can pursue purity so as to secure harmony and happiness in my interactions with other people. I can give myself wholly with no reserves to learning, teaching, communicating, contributing, sacrificing, and creating enjoyable encounters with others through my many roles as a person. A friend. A relative. A recording artist. A podcaster. An author. An actor. An inventor or influencer. A counselor. A Christian. I can be all of these things for their benefit and relief, to serve others and to prioritize their needs. I can cultivate an environment that's easy for others to exist in and find a trustworthy solace in a world that can leave us scared and skittish by broken promises, disappointments, and unexpected inconveniences.

I can confess sin and not hide it because of having to keep up a facade that I am ever progressing and climbing upward on the ladder to heaven. I don't have to keep lowering the standard to pretend I am somewhere or someone that I am not. I can be regularly pursuing growth and God's way, knowing and resting in the fact that my salvation does not depend on that growth.

My growth and efforts to press onward toward God's good way are the result of His Spirit working in me, and I am free to travel down that path, knowing that God has made it clear for me because it's safe and is God's best for me. Even when I don't understand it all and am perplexed by the unexpected, I can rest in the character and nature of God, who has a perfect knowledge of me. He knows my limits, my upbringing, my intellectual capacity, and my quirks. He considers all of who I am and engages me accordingly, for my good.

I can trust God's promise to forgive, seeing that He has gone out of His way to overwhelm us with hugs of grace and forgiveness. He delights in kissing us with the purest Fatherly affection in absolution. He has opened up the windows of heaven and poured out much grace on us. Not only that, He is the one who condescends to come to us from without. He comes to visit us in many ways to lavish us with more and more grace and forgiveness. **Everywhere you turn, there is Good News there.** Good News specifically for you. Specifically for me, FLAME.

CHAPTER 10

WORD AND WATER

Another way God personally comes to us with forgiveness and provides ongoing assurance is Baptism. This idea was foreign to me because, like most Christians influenced by contemporary Evangelicalism, I understood Baptism to be an outward sign of an inward change. That's simply what's handed down to you as a kid. Although kids are mostly spectators when it comes to Baptism, unfortunately. We shall discuss that later.

I had never heard of baptismal regeneration. Or to say it differently, I never heard that God uses Baptism to save. Even typing it just now made me chuckle because it took a lot for me to get here. It was such a strange and unusual concept at first. How can Baptism save? Where in the Bible does it say that? How can a work that I perform save me? *These Lutherans are tripping and teaching false doctrines*, I thought.

The typical way Baptism was taught in my previous context is that after people hear the message that they are sinners and must turn away from their sin and toward God in repentance, then they should get baptized as an outward sign to the world that they are serious about God and ready to leave their worldly ways and live for Jesus.

After people repent of their sins, then they join the church and take a new member class. During the new member class, they learn some foundational things about the faith. Once the class is completed, they sign up to get baptized. This is scheduled, and people may prepare a brief spiel, a testimony/conversion story to read or recite from memory to the congregation.

When that exciting day rolls around, the new members are draped in white robes and briefed by the pastor in the back room on the order of events. As they approach the baptismal pool, the nerves are dancing. They are going over their testimonies to make sure they don't mess up when they say it aloud. The time has come. The pastor summons each person forward to approach the tub.

With microphone in hand, the pastor says a few words to the congregation about the joy of seeing brother or sister "so-and-so" giving his or her life to the Lord. He may tell a funny story about how the person was before salvation and how much he or she changed in just a few weeks. Then, the pastor invites the person to say a few words—hopefully only the ones the pastor approved in advance.

The person reads the spiel, and tears start to flow, recalling how God has saved him and changed his heart. The pastor grabs the mic back and says, "[So-and-so,] I now baptize you in the name of the Father, the Son, and the Holy Spirit." No sign of the cross is made across the heart because that's perceived to be Roman Catholic. The pastor dips the person in the water and draws him out of the water, and the church erupts with applause and praise, happy to see "so-and-so" now baptized.

This is the normal order of events surrounding Baptism in the generic American church. After that, your Baptism is most likely never brought up again, never discussed or seen as relevant again. There are only two other occasions when your Baptism is discussed: (1) if, years later, you backslide, depart from church membership, or leave Christianity altogether, and (2) your Baptism may get an honorable mention at your funeral, maybe. The pastor may remind people that you got baptized before and that you were a great person.

Other than that, it's a forgotten event. It's like runners at the starting line. Once they take off, they never think of the starting line again. The goal is to get to the finish line, and that's it. No one cares about the starting line. Yep, this is predictable trajectory for Baptism talk. Correct me if I'm wrong. However, after having this topic presented again to me, I had to wrestle with it again.

Through vigorous wrestling with the teaching of baptismal regeneration, I now see what the ancient Church saw from the days of the New Testament and rejoice with the saints of old. Now, having my mind rightfully rewired concerning Baptism, I see it and experience it in its proper light, and it's beautiful! God just can't stop giving us love and comfort and grace through regular earthy means.

In my short project titled *Word and Water*, I set out to help define and unpack what the Bible actually says about Baptism. In the song titled "He Delivers," this is how we as confessional Lutherans confess and articulate what God says He is doing in Baptism.

It reads:

Baptism is God's promise coupled with the water
where He promises to give us all the
benefits we get from crucifixion
like forgiveness of our sins, hold up.
If you will it's like irrigation
delivering grace and salvation
a Sacrament that He instituted He can freely do it
He is God ain't He.
It's a work that He does for us
me boy
and our faith just receives it
trust me boy
but that faith is gift He gave us
me boy
I'm not making this up
look it up me boy.
"Unless one is born of the water and Spirit
then how can he enter the kingdom of God?"
So He baptized us in the triune name
Holy Spirit, the Son, the Father.
Selah
When I'm doubting my faith and I'm stuck in my head
then I look outside to the promise He gives
that Baptism saves
was buried and rose up with Christ

that's what our Baptism is
and everything Jesus' Baptism did
we benefit 'cause our Baptism's in His.
The Spirit, forgiveness, Jesus' perfection, resurrection,
the Word and the water gives.

Two important realities to point out from this verse are that Baptism is the water and the Word of God combined and that Baptism is God's work, not ours. As St. Augustine describes it, a sacrament is an earthly element and the Word of God. This is what Scripture reveals as Jesus Himself establishes the Sacraments for us to observe. Therefore, Baptism is the earthly element of water coupled with God's Word of promise, His promise to wash away our sins.

Paul says in Ephesians 5:25–27:

> Husbands, love your wives, as Christ loved the
> church and gave Himself up for her, that He might
> sanctify her, having cleansed her by the washing
> of water with the word, so that He might present
> the church to Himself in splendor, without spot or
> wrinkle or any such thing, that she might be holy
> and without blemish.

It should be noted that the pronoun *her* in this text is the Church. Jesus says He is sanctifying her, cleansing her, presenting her to Himself in splendor without spot or wrinkle that the Church might be holy and without blemish. How is He doing that according to this text? By washing of water with the Word. That is Baptism. The text is careful to point out that it is Jesus Himself who is doing the baptizing. He is the one doing the verbs. He is the one doing the work. Baptism is God's work that He does for us. Not the other way around.

This can be hard for many to hear. Not only because of how we've been taught but also because the old Adam in us delights in striving to earn salvation. We love a good law or a good rule to try and keep. It's how we are wired. It's how the world functions. You work hard in school, you can earn an A+. You work hard at your job and earn your money. You work harder and earn a raise. And so it goes. So to hear that Baptism is God's work and not ours feels unnatural. Just like the message of the preached Gospel: trust in Jesus' work on the cross for you by faith. We think, *Wait, what's the catch? So we just passively receive and don't get to earn our way to heaven? Nah, that doesn't feel right*, the old Adam in us says.

So for us to admit that we got Baptism wrong by relegating it to our first act of obedience feels counterintuitive. There's an old Adam–size void in us that feels empty confessing that. Therefore, it's helpful to breathe and pray for an open heart to reconsider Baptism objectively, based on the Scriptures. For that reason, I made this request in a verse from "Why Wait":

> *Take a minute read the Scriptures on Baptism*
> *without your presuppositions*
> *and the washings in the Old Testament*
> *like Naaman washed in the Jordan River.*

Don't forget the Levitical priestly washings and
Ezekiel's vision
you get the picture from the Scripture that Baptism
is now the fulfillment (connect that).
Sometimes water drowns
God use it to judge.
Sometimes water saves
think of Noah's flood.
They in the boat
the boat was floating
window opened
then Noah sent out a dove
the second time the dove came in
in her mouth was an olive leaf freshly plucked.
Peter said they were saved through the water
like Israel was saved through the water
when Moses split the Red Sea
He [God] judged some
and made sons and daughters (out of others).
It's by faith it's not magic.
Don't have faith you can't access
forgiveness
if you resist
then that's it
but if it's repentance happening by the Spirit
then I'm asking.

If by God's Spirit we can exercise the discipline of laying down our inherited presuppositions and objectively seeing what God has been up to since the origin of creation with water and His Holy Spirit, then maybe we can rightly dive into the ocean of His grace and be eternally refreshed. Peter certainly wants us to know this forgiveness delivered through Baptism. He says it plainly in 1 Peter 3:20–21:

> Because they formerly did not obey, when God's patience waited in the days of Noah, while the ark was being prepared, in which a few, that is, eight persons, were brought safely through water. Baptism, which corresponds to this, now saves you, not as a removal of dirt from the body but as an appeal to God for a good conscience, through the resurrection of Jesus Christ.

In the same way eight persons "were brought safely through water," Baptism now saves us. It is one of God's many means to deliver His grace to us. Note, Lutherans are not saying that Baptism is the only way to receive salvation. We do not teach sola Baptism, that Baptism alone saves. Yet Scripture confesses that it is a Means of Grace—a means of deliverance unto salvation.

However, it is not magic. When done in the triune name of God the Father, God the Son, and God the Holy Spirit, He is present in and with the water to deliver His grace and to bestow faith. However, a person can reject that faith and the Holy Spirit, the promised gifts of Baptism. If the person is an atheist but is only going through the ritual to quiet his mom's pestering, then he will not receive the benefits of what's available to him in the Baptism because he is immediately rejecting it. Yet if he repented of his sin later on in life and wanted to become a Christian, he would not need to be baptized again. I'll say it again: Baptism is the work of God. Not ours. That person should simply return to his Baptism and receive the benefits, meaning that he can be confident that when he was baptized, God was present with grace and forgiveness.

Now by faith, we can lay hold of the promise God made in our Baptism. Remember, the Bible says God is faithful even when we are not. In addition, Paul says there is one Lord, one faith, and one Baptism. A rebaptizing is unnecessary. However, if the person's conscience is troubling them, then he can meet privately with his pastor for further discussion on the true nature of Baptism and the best way forward.

People oftentimes jokingly say, "Well if that's the case, how about we go around with water guns randomly spraying water on complete strangers while yelling out from a safe distance, 'I now baptize you in the name of the Father, Son, and Holy Spirit! Too late now, you're a Christian! And heaven bound!!'" I admit, that sounds hilariously fun and would make for great viral content. Nevertheless, there's no biblical criterion for such outlandish behavior. Since people can reject faith, this is not a helpful solution and will probably cause more harm than good.

"Well, what about the thief of the cross?" people fire back. "He wasn't baptized, and Jesus said I'll see you in heaven in a few minutes." To this, we reply with a reminder that Lutherans do not teach Baptism only or that Baptism alone saves. A person can be saved by the reading of the Word. By the hearing of the Word.

Or by the visible Word—Baptism, in this case. Here, there is the temptation to pit one Scripture passage against the other as if one will cancel the other one out. That's the wrong thing to do. The Bible does not contradict itself. The Bible is consistent with itself and is in full harmony of thought and theology. From Genesis to Revelation, there are no contradictions at all. Therefore, we must ask, "How do we harmonize these two texts?" Not "Let's pick one and unleash a nuclear attack on the other." **This means the thief on the cross was saved by hearing Jesus' words of promise the same way a person trusts in Jesus' words of promise through His other means.**

After all, Jesus says this in Mark 16:16:

> Whoever believes and is baptized will be saved, but whoever does not believe will be condemned.

Jesus ties Baptism and salvation together, but in the second portion of this text, He says, "Whoever does not believe will be condemned." It's safe to conclude that Baptism saves, but if one is not afforded the opportunity for some reason, they can still be saved by believing in Jesus' Word. In all actuality, the thief on the cross received exactly what we receive in Baptism: a clear and sure word from Jesus that we will be saved and with Him in paradise. Same Word, delivered in different ways. One by hearing. One by the visible Word, Baptism.

JESUS VERSUS BAPTISM? NOT AT ALL

One person said this to me after hearing me celebrate what God does for us in the Sacrament of Baptism that He established:

"FLAME, you're glorifying Baptism more than Jesus!"

I replied, "God always uses physical means to deliver His gifts. The eternal Son of God took on human flesh (physicality) to save us."

If that same God-man says in John 3:5, "Truly, truly, I say to you, unless one is born of water and the Spirit, he cannot enter the kingdom of God" and then in Mark 16:16, "Whoever believes and is baptized will be saved, but whoever does not believe will be condemned," then it follows that Jesus Himself is being glorified in Baptism. There's no necessary competition between God and His ordained means.

No one ever says there's competition between the preincarnate Son—Christ before He permanently took on human flesh—and the incarnate Jesus. The very notion is absurd. We embrace the God-man as the physical and divine "means" whereby He, Himself, saves us.

In like manner, God's Spirit is "in and with" the waters of Baptism.

These things only sound foreign to us because we are on the other side of the Enlightenment. Although, as mentioned before, the majority of Christians living today from the Eastern and the Western Church do not hold to a symbolic view of Baptism but to baptismal regeneration. For those of us who hold to baptismal regeneration, we are not only in alignment with what God revealed in His Word but also with what the earliest of Christians held to. In a song titled "The Patristics" from my *Word and Water* EP, I provided this evidence:

[Hook]
Irenaeus taught it
Athanasius taught it
Even Origen taught it
Cyprian of Carthage taught it
and Chrysostom taught it
St. Augustine taught it
The Martyr Justin taught it
Hippolytus taught it
Basil the Great taught it
The Didache taught it
Nicene Creed taught it
and Ambrose, yeah, he taught it
and Jerome taught it
Cyril of Jerusalem taught it
Paul and Peter taught it
because Jesus taught it.
[Verse 1]
Family it's clearly unanimous
Baptism truly is regenerative.
Go study them early Patristics (like Clement and
Polycarp)
the position is really ubiquitous.
He told me we're giving tradition too much authority
let's see what the Bible says
then he started quoting his denomination's tradition
to see what the Bible says.

I told him the goal was lookin' at those
who wrote closer to the first century
to see what they taught on the topic
they were not as far removed as you and me.
Then you discovered the fact
some of the early text
some of them dating back
AD 80, facts.
People like the Shepherd Hermas
taught Baptism's where He saves us at.
Then you find people like Origen
third century and even that boy taught it.
Then here comes Zwingli again
swinging again to the other extreme
changing unanimous things
the Church believed for the first 1600 (years).
[Hook]
[Verse 2]
You're simply not going to find
not one Church Father that made the confession
that what Baptism really is
an outward sign of an inward expression.
It's not in the Bible and Scripture don't teach it.
American pulpits
most people preach it.
Wanna know what Baptism really is

1 Peter 3 verse 20, 21
go read it.
Baptism saves remission of sins
a Means of Grace to get you cleansed.
Faith receives it based on Jesus' work
the ancient Church believed it.
Why you think some delayed Baptism.
No Cap like Cappadocian Fathers
believed so much Baptism did save
just to be safe they'd push it back farther.
Even people liked Tertullian believed that the act of
Baptism did save.
The man didn't believe original sin
so bypass baby Baptism and do it later.
Yes we repent receive by faith
forgiveness connect to Means of Grace.
The Word and water will clean our slate.
Read Acts chapter 2 verse 38, 39.
Selah

The Acts 2 reference made certain brothers and sisters in the Lord from the more Charismatic side of things raise an eyebrow. Many of them suggest that the Bible is not keen on water Baptism but rather "Spirit Baptism." In short, Spirit Baptism is the idea that there are two aspects of the Christian faith, that this "second blessing" that comes later, after initial salvation, is a superior experience to simply being a regular water-baptized Christian. Yes, there is a difference between John's Baptism and the Baptism of the Holy Spirit fulfilled at Pentecost. Nevertheless, that does not make water Baptism inferior to the miraculous phenomena that followed the giving of the Holy Spirit at Pentecost. This confusion can be attributed to a misunderstanding of the nature of the Book of Acts.

THE BOOK OF ACTS IS UNIQUE

The term "redemptive historic uniqueness" is used to describe the nature of the Book of Acts. The events that take place throughout the book are unique to this transitional time in redemptive history. In particular, Pentecost and the mini-Pentecosts that happen throughout the Book of Acts culminate as a statement of unity and diversity in Christ as one Body. This event marks the origin of the Christian Church, which is made up not only of Jews but of all nations, tribes, and tongues united by the outpouring of the Holy Spirit at Pentecost.

The reality that the Book of Acts is unique in nature is not a statement meant to dismiss the gifts of the Spirit. God is free to bestow gifts and perform miracles at His own prerogative and to whom He pleases. I am by no means arguing that the gifts have ceased. That is not the intention of this discussion.

Having said that, there is an unhealthy and unbiblical school of thought lurking among Christian thinking that some believers in Christ are living beneath and without all that God has for them by way of supernatural experiences and abilities. Make no mistake, you are not missing out on the "fullness of Christ" if you have not spoken in tongues or prophesied or performed or experienced healings and miracles.

In fact, 2 Peter 1:3 says:

> His divine power has granted to us all things that
> pertain to life and godliness.

This we have in Christ alone. You are not missing anything. Do not let anyone convince you otherwise or pressure you into thinking less of yourself as a baptized believer.

WHY THE FUSS?

The point of conflict resides with the varying order of things related to Baptism and the giving of the Holy Spirit. There are occasions where the giving of the Holy Spirit is included in Baptism, as in Acts 2:38–39. There were also occasions when persons were baptized and had not yet received the Holy Spirit until hands were laid on them by the apostles, as in Acts 8:12–17. There are also occasions such as Acts 10:44–48, when the Holy Spirit fell on the Gentiles, coupled with the gift of tongues, first, and then Baptism followed. These three varying scenarios should be understood with the term "redemptive historic uniqueness." That term demonstrates the "wildness" of this holy phenomenon.

It should also be pointed out that the giving of the Spirit was performed by the apostles themselves by the laying on of hands, or at least in their presence, and with an insistence on binding things together. There is an urgency by the apostles to unite Baptism and the giving of the Holy Spirit. They never settled for one experience or the other. They always made sure, regardless of the order of things, to unite them all together, almost as if to say, "Let's rightly orient these things."

That's the norm that should be highlighted. Not the contemporary rhetoric, by some, that tongues must follow the possession of the Holy Spirit each time without exception. Furthermore, at one of the mini-Pentecosts in Acts 8:14–17, the expression of tongues—languages, not gibberish—did not follow the giving of the Holy Spirit. Peter and John made no fuss about that nor demanded it as a result of the giving of the Holy Spirit.

Yes, verse 13 says:

> Even Simon himself believed, and after being
> baptized he continued with Philip. And
> seeing signs and great miracles performed, he
> was amazed.

Yet it does not say one of those signs or miracles was tongues. To argue from silence that tongues was one of the accompanying amazements would be an error, a thing to avoid.

After the Book of Acts, the normal pattern of things rises to the surface. What we observe from the Epistles is Baptism rightly oriented as a Means of Grace whereby the Holy Spirit saves and sanctifies. No longer do we observe the activities that followed Pentecost or the few mini-Pentecosts from the Book of Acts. Again, that is not to say God has ceased to perform miracles in our world.

These passages demonstrate the relationship between Baptism, the Holy Spirit, salvation, and sanctification: Romans 6:1–5; Galatians 3:27; Ephesians 5:25–27; Colossians 11–12; Titus 3:5; 1 Peter 3:20–21.

Titus 3:5 says this:

> He saved us, not because of works done by us in
> righteousness, but according to His own mercy, by
> the washing of regeneration and renewal of the
> Holy Spirit.

It is clear that the Book of Acts is unique. It is also clear that the remaining books in the New Testament do not demand the activities that followed the giving of the Holy Spirit be repeated or duplicated. One should now be relieved of any added burdens of having to achieve higher levels of spiritual manifestations. The added burden of insecurities that you are not one of God's special ones or one of His favorites. The false notion that having Christ's presence in your life is not enough but that the second Spirit Baptism is the fullness of the Gospel. All those thoughts can be properly put away and buried in the ground forever. We are justified by Christ alone. Water Baptism is sufficient. God is free to act and to distribute gifts and miracles when and upon whom He wills.

REAL WATER

Many have contended with me that "Spirit Baptism" cancels out water Baptism altogether. That was a new one for me. I responded to one person this way:

First, Jesus was baptized in real water. Matthew 3:16:

> And when Jesus was baptized, immediately He
> went up from the water, and behold, the heavens
> were opened to Him, and He saw the Spirit of God
> descending like a dove and coming to rest on Him.

Second, the Ethiopian eunuch was baptized in real water. Acts 8:36:

> And as they were going along the road they came to some water, and the eunuch said, "See, here is water! What prevents me from being baptized?"

Third, Peter used real water to baptize the believing Gentiles. Acts 10:47:

> Can anyone withhold water for baptizing these people, who have received the Holy Spirit just as we have?

The Holy Spirit accompanies the water in Baptism. The Holy Spirit and His work using real water is a theme in the Bible. At the origin of creation, the Holy Spirit hovered over the waters. Creation was born from water and the Spirit (and the entire triune presence, including the Word, Jesus). Also, John 7:38–39 is speaking about Jesus giving the Holy Spirit. At this point, the Spirit had not yet been given. After Jesus' death, this was fulfilled at Pentecost.

John 7:38:

> Whoever believes in Me, as the Scripture has said, "Out of his heart will flow rivers of living water."

This sentence is in reference to the Holy Spirit. That's perfectly fine. No argument there. Yet this does not cancel out Baptism being with real water. That's a leap. You must let both realities exist. You can't cancel out the use of real water because of the usage here.

Furthermore:

> According to John's understanding the rivers of living water meant "the Spirit which they that believed on Him were to receive." That Spirit comes from Christ, the "fountain of the Spirit" as Irenaeus calls Him, and therefore the words "out of his belly" must not be referred to the individual believer, nor even, in the first place, to the Church, the body of Christ, but to Christ Himself, the Rock (see 1 Corinth. 10:4) of whom it was said (Exodus 17:6): "Thou shalt smite the Rock and there shall come from within it waters, and the people shall drink." This meaning of the passage becomes very clear if we adopt a different punctuation, reading as follows, without the slightest change of the original: "If any man thirst let him come (unto Me) and let him that believeth on me, drink; as it is written."[8]

INFANT BAPTISM

The blessings of Baptism can be explored endlessly. God nurtures us from the cradle to the grave in His baptismal gifts. Yes, even infants receive the gifts of Baptism. Consider these words from my song "Mark Them":

[Hook]
Ooo yea
Marks them with the triune name
Ooo yea
forgives them of sin then makes them clean.
Ooo yea
Get the Spirit and the gift of faith at once

---

8   Adolph Spaeth, *Annotations on the Gospel According to St. John* (n.p.: Just and Sinner Publications, 2019), 122.

Ooo yea
bring them babies to the font.
Ooo yea
Mark them with the triune name
Ooo yea
Baptism saves, come get them clean.
Ooo yea
Get the Spirit and the gift of faith at once
Ooo yea
bring them babies to the font.
[Verse 1]
I know that you think it's impossible
you see an obstacle
how can an infant perceive
how can a baby be making professions of faith
when they can't repent and believe (cause faith is a gift).
Assuming we value the Bible (it's God's work)
Jesus said go make disciples (not our work)
by baptizing all the nations (He baptizes)
that means no discrimination (all ages).
What He didn't say is
you had to be from a certain place to get the benefit.
What He didn't say is
you had to be of a certain age to get the benefit.
What He did do
rebuke the disciples from keeping the children away
from Him.

Matter of fact He said
become like the children if you want to enter (the
kingdom of God).
Speaking of faith
babies can definitely have faith
man it's all over the Psalms.
Psalm 22
Psalm 71
trusted in God while he's nursing on moms.
This for the skeptics who still need to sign
hit the New Testament go look at John.
Mary visited Elizabeth
he was filled with the Spirit
even before he was born.
[Hook]
[Verse 2]
Speaking of infants in the Old Testament
yes they were a part of the family of God.
To be an Israelite
go get a knife
the sons getting circumcised.
Through it they entered the family of faith.
See the connection the apostle made.
Go to Colossians 2:11, 12
it's Baptism that is literally delivering grace (it's more
inclusive).

191

Okay let me set the precedent (it's reasonable).
Take a look at the New Testament (to think that is true).
Let us begin with the Book of Acts
and the household passages in the text.
Peter was preaching a sermon at Pentecost
people start feeling the weight of the Law
about the murder of Jesus they caused
when they heard it they were cut to the heart.
Then they said what should we do.
Repent and be baptized for the forgiveness of sins
receive the gift of the Spirit this promise for you
and is for all of your kids.
Think about Lydia
think of Cornelius
Stephanas
and the Philippian jailer.
All of them baptized
even their households
including babies receive a Savior.

I think it's particularly profound that in Luke 18:15–17, Jesus calls adults to be more like children to enter the kingdom of God. He does not call children to be more like adults. Children are the quintessential example of trust and passive receiving of gifts. It's what they know best. So it is in Baptism. An infant heeds the voice of their Savior and is given the gift of faith and thus inherits eternal life. **According to Jesus, adults must learn to be like the infant.**

MY HEART

I was baptized around four or five years old but was talked out of considering it as legitimate. The next time I went under the water, I was told that it was because I demonstrated necessary fruit, which proved I was ready to finally be baptized. As far back as I can remember, my experience with Christianity has been riddled with blurred lines between resting in Christ and working to maintain my salvation. I suppose over time, I just got tired. Understandably so, now knowing what I know.

This makes my heart go out to all those who are stuck in that same cycle I was. I think about them often and pray for Christians who have never encountered the things I've discovered in the Lutheran tradition that took me back to the purity of the Bible and the rest that we have in Christ. The more I got to know about Martin Luther and his colleague Philip Melanchthon, I felt we shared kindred spirits, as they were fighting for some of the same things in their day that I am passionate about.

MISUSE OF SCRIPTURE CRUSHES THE PEOPLE

The Word of God in the wrong hands will always have grave consequences. History testifies that this is certainly the case. Considering that, my affections are always drawn toward the people—the innocent onlookers who are at the mercy of those with the platform and influence, the seekers of God who simply want to know how to be made right with Him. It's that simple.

Yet they are often at a disadvantage, having little exposure and knowledge about the Bible, the original languages of holy writ, and the historical background of biblical history. Therefore, the person who appears to have that knowledge will take the lead and be exalted, especially if they have the "right look," holy garbs, and a charismatic personality with winsome speaking abilities.

Article XIIb on the misuses of Scripture in the Apology of the Augsburg Confession confronts this reality. The medieval Roman Catholic Church, much like many contemporary denominations, struggled with bending the biblical meaning of many texts. Such compromises always add a burden to one's faith and fracture the conscience. Inherently, the people will be taught, in one way or another, that they must exhaust much effort with high-quality performance to earn God's favor.

As mentioned, my theological roots are from the Charismatic and Prosperity denominations. While good foundational truths were preserved there, alongside of those are notions of winning God's blessings. One must sincerely praise God aloud or sacrificially give a financial gift in order to be blessed.

For example, Malachi 3:7–10 was a go-to text to persuade us to give more money to be blessed:

> From the days of your fathers you have turned
> aside from My statutes and have not kept them.
> Return to Me, and I will return to you, says the
> LORD of hosts. But you say, "How shall we return?"
> Will man rob God? Yet you are robbing Me. But
> you say, "How have we robbed You?" In your tithes
> and contributions. You are cursed with a curse, for
> you are robbing Me, the whole nation of you. Bring
> the full tithe into the storehouse, that there may
> be food in My house. And thereby put Me to the

test, says the LORD of hosts, if I will not open the
windows of heaven for you and pour down for you
a blessing until there is no more need.

Completely ignored is the context of the Book of Malachi. God
was addressing the entire nation of Israel. He was confronting their
lack of faith expressed in little financial support of the Levitical
priests. He was not offering tips to acquire a bigger bank account,
nor was He establishing a universal principle that if you give until
it hurts your wallet or purse that God is obligated to bless you one
hundredfold.

**What often happens is this: if a person gives sacrificially
and isn't blessed in their desired way, their consciences become
severely troubled.** One is left with mounds of doubt and deep
wonderings of whether or not God is pleased with them. If they
gave cheerfully but did not get the car they wanted, perhaps God
was punishing them for some unknown sin. From there, the person
begins to confess all known sin and their lack of faith. Next, they
begin to search deeply for any unknown trespasses. They might
even make vows to never indulge in a sin again, in hopes to move
God's hand. And so it goes.

A similar system was in place during Luther's day. To earn
God's forgiveness, a person was expected to confess all their sins
and to demonstrate to God through acts of satisfaction that they
were genuinely sorry for their wrongs. Indulgences, too, consisted
of making a financial contribution for the sake of earning God's
blessings. In addition, although a person may have been absolved
during Confession and Absolution, one was still burdened with

the task of canonical satisfactions and plenty of other works to complete the repentance process.

Furthermore, Rome insisted that "the apostles preach repentance; therefore, eternal punishments are relieved by the punishments of purgatory; therefore, the Keys have the power to pardon part of the punishments of purgatory; therefore, satisfactions deliver from the punishments of purgatory!"[9] Layers and layers of human works intended to satisfy God's wrath. All to the exclusion of Jesus' finished work on the cross for us.

Essential to Luther and Melanchthon's concern was the Word of God being accurately taught for the sake of healing troubled consciences. What they rightly understood was that adding anything to the completed work of Jesus was to lose the Gospel. To lose the Gospel necessarily leaves a person buried underneath the crushing weight of the Law. Hence their insistence upon Christ alone as the conqueror of sin, Satan, and death itself.

Rome insisted that the Lutheran Reformers were a threat to good works, insisting that their rhetoric would lead to lawlessness. However, Melanchthon was careful to articulate the falsity of their concern. He echoed Jesus and the New Testament authors that good works are the result of God's saving work. After listing a host of good works, Melanchthon was careful to mention the fruit that Christians bear is "not for a repayment of eternal punishment, but so as not to obey the devil or offend the Holy Spirit."[10]

Neither Luther nor Melanchthon was an advocate for

---

9 Apology of the Augsburg Confession, Article XIIB, 26.

10 Apology of the Augsburg Confession, Article XIIB, 77.

lawlessness. They simply sought to properly orient salvation as a free gift won by Jesus and good works as the result of the free gift of grace. Not the cause. Satisfactions, purgatory, and indulgences are not means of salvation. When a congregant is absolved, there are no tasks left to fulfill. Jesus fulfilled the ones the Father required for us.

Even traditions that teach justification by faith alone should be cautious with how they arrange sanctification in the room lest they, too, wind up nearer to medieval Rome than they thought. If progressive sanctification is positioned equally and parallel to objective justification as proof of salvation, one may blur the lines and unknowingly mingle good works and grace, further troubling the conscience and causing many to stumble. Parishioners should know that we actively perform good works for the benefit of our neighbor, yet we are passively accounted as righteous for Christ's sake.

LIVING IN THE POWER OF MY BAPTISM

One should not hear that Lutherans do not value godliness or good works. That would be to misunderstand everything written in this book as well as everything written in the Book of Concord, which are the Lutheran Confessions. As argued above, the original Reformers were sensitively conscientious toward having good works rightly oriented. Rightfully so, they sought to safeguard the purity of the Gospel to the point of risking life and limb.

Lutherans live in the reality that we are baptized. **We don't view our Baptism as something in the past. It is indeed our identity. We rightly acknowledge that as the baptized, we live**

a life of repentance. Our lives are ever in the motion of Baptism: dying to sin and rising to life, grace, and forgiveness.

As a final poetic expression of my journey, I submit to you my song titled "Let Us Remember":

Let us Lord
let us remember
let us remember
it's the water and Your Word
You gave to cleanse us
You gave to cleanse us.
You made us brand new oh Lord
thank You for bringing us close
so let us Lord
let us remember
remember.
[Verse 1]
God, I tried
tried to scuba dive
tried to plumb the depths
in the ocean of affections and it left me out of breath.
God I tried
tried to stay in line
perfectly in step
tried to keep Your marching orders but my heart kept
going left.

I said God
I'm trying to survive
my conscious is wrecked
it's a mess
I need strength
trying to live this life in the flesh.
This is why
need to look outside
outside of yourself
for your help.
If your faith's in God
and you've been baptized
then you're blessed
you possess
victory over devil death
forgiveness
God's grace
triune God and His gifts.
To Your Word I cling
continue in sin
by no means
Romans 6 baptized in Him
I rise with Him
so I'm clean.
Extra nos.
[Hook]

[Verse 2]
Now I can put that old Adam down.
Water and the Word make that old Adam drown.
When I see him swimming back around
Spirit working in me now
He spinning on them now (whoa).
You say how can water keep your soul in order.
I say that's a part of it but it's more than water.
It's the Word of God in and with the water.
Without faith and His Word it's just plain water.
Paul taught us
about a washing in Titus 3 and 5
whereby the Spirit regenerates us and saves lives.
We just lend our limbs
but it's Him
doing the baptizing
sweet Sacrament
where God acts
outside of us.

Matters of assurance are near to my heart. Maybe it's my personality, or maybe it's all the things I've gone through in life. I am profoundly in touch with our need to know we are right with God. Life is hard, and I believe the last thing we need is to live predominately in fear and anxiety concerning our standing with Him. In 2020, my mom went to be with the Lord. I was grateful that I was able to spend the last two weeks of her life by her bedside.

Even as I write this, my eyes are welling up with tears. I am her only child, so we shared a special bond. I remember throughout her life, we would talk about issues of assurance. We'd always land on trusting in Jesus and what He did for us on the cross. **All of us can experience moments of profound doubt about our salvation and simply hope that our good will outweigh our bad.**

I'm grateful that I got to share the wonderful news with my mom about how God has gone out of His way to bless us in a multiplicity of ways to know He is for us. She was my number-one fan and loved my *Extra Nos* EP. She kept my music on her computer so she could hear my voice while I was out and about. She was deeply comforted by the things God allowed me to share with her. For that, I am grateful. Although I'm sure she could tell me a thing or two about how much God is for us, now that she is present with the Lord.

While grieving the loss of my dear mom, ten months later, my beloved dad went to be with the Lord also. They were high school sweethearts. They were relatively young. My mom had just turned sixty and my dad was sixty-six. They were married close to thirty years but had been together since they were teens. I was truly blessed to have them as parents.

Although I was not able to spend time with my dad during his final hours, he left me something special. My cousin found a handwritten letter he wrote me and mailed it to my house. In that letter, he told me that although we lost Mom, we can take heart that she is with the Lord and the rest of our family members. He told me it was okay to cry and to know how much they both love me. He concluded the letter by telling me to stay the course and to keep trusting in Christ Jesus, our Lord.

He was certainly a proud dad and was my second number-one fan. Both he and my mom would quote my lyrics and rap my songs. It was so funny! I celebrate that they shared in the joy of salvation with me. I'm glad they both were able to be exposed to the sweet assurance that God saw fit to deliver to us in many ways. Not only did my dad love the *Extra Nos* EP but he got to hear *Christ for You*, too, and loved it. Now that they both are present with the Lord, I get to continue their legacy of sharing the hope of the Gospel with the world. God is good.

It's not lost on me that others are currently grieving and dealing with the difficulties of life. Some are simply tired and ready to punt the faith altogether. Others are persevering in the faith but scrambling to find inspiration to hope again. There are many who are wrestling with vices but want help and are stuck in a pit of despair. Others are tempted to believe the devil's lie that God will never forgive them because their sin is too great. Many are looking for a word to cling to—a specific word from God to help them overcome temptation, doubt, or spiritual fatigue. Many are looking for a recharge by being baptized again, hoping that would give them the boost they need. People are changing churches or skipping out on meeting with the saints completely.

All these matters are not beyond the scope of God's care and consideration. This is precisely what salvation being extra nos, outside of us, is all about. This is what God's Word and the Sacraments are all about. In these times of doubt, you have the Lord's Supper, where Jesus visits us with forgiveness, renewal, and strength. At the Lord's Table, He applies immortality to us. He unites us afresh with Himself and with all the saints—those who are living and those living with Him (John 6).

In these times of doubt, Baptism helps uniquely. You can count on the fact that you are baptized. Your head received the water and God's Word of promise done in the triune name of God. That's His particular Word to you: That He will save you. That He is for you and will never leave you nor turn His back on you.

After Jesus' resurrection, in Matthew 28:16–20, the Bible says some doubted. Jesus came to them and said, "I have all authority in heaven and on earth, now go baptize and teach people my words and behold that I will be with you always even to the end of the age."

Jesus chose to comfort people's doubts with Baptism and His Word, His Word of forgiveness, hope, assurance, and a vow to always be with us to the end.

So when you are tempted to believe your inner voice over God's Word, remind yourself that you are baptized. When you are tempted to forget who you are and to act out of character, you can recall your Baptism. Say to yourself, "I am a baptized child of God, let me think or do otherwise."

CHAPTER 11

A PRAYER

Dear Father, I pray for all those reading or hearing this book. I ask that You would bring comfort to those who are secretly afraid that You don't like them anymore. I pray for those who don't feel good enough and can't imagine that You still love them. I think of the many who have left Christianity recently for one reason or another but commonly felt hurt, lost, or confused by life's conditions.

I ask that You would meet them where they are with whispers of Your love and kindness.

That You would draw them back into Your fold.

That they would hear of Your grace and forgiveness and would be compelled, by Your Spirit, to trust You again, to return to their Baptism where You delivered Your gifts.

I ask that many who have never heard of what You are doing for us, outside of us, by faith alone and not our work, would lean into these realities and find rest for their troubled consciences. I pray that the sweet sacramental truths as articulated through Lutheran thought would not be repelling to them, but that they would recognize in them Your voice.

I pray that they would hear not only of Your universal expression of love by sending Your Son, Jesus, to die for us all on the cross but that they would know Your love is particular, as demonstrated by Your Son's bodily presence in the bread and the wine—for them in particular by name.

I ask that they would know that same assurance by remembering their Baptism and the gift of salvation You delivered to them, in particular, in the water and Word, by name. I ask that these truths would liberate those who are exhausted and discouraged, depressed, or stuck in a particular pattern of sin. Let these wonderful teachings lead them to passion for life and good works unto neighbor. In Your Son Jesus' name I ask. Amen.

ACKNOWLEDGMENTS

I must acknowledge those who helped the Lutheran world make sense to me while I was being newly exposed to it, those who led me back to Scripture and a right understanding of it. Thank you, Concordia Seminary, St. Louis, and all my professors who helped me reconsider Christianity. The joy I experienced during my time on campus continues to pervade my soul. The levels of appreciation cannot be expressed in words. Jordan Cooper, thank you for your tireless labor and visible presence on social media and YouTube while I was exploring and learning early on. I still learn from you. Wittenberg Project, thank you all for being relevant and relatable influencers on YouTube, heralding Lutheran thought as young Black males. This contributed greatly to my journey. Thank you, "Ask the Pastor" from Holy Cross Lutheran Church. Your videos on YouTube helped me ponder the Scriptures and were, and continue to be, a deep source of renewal. Concordia Publishing House, I thank you all for giving me the opportunity to produce this work and share the wonderful tradition of confessional Lutheran thought with the world—in essence, to share Jesus and His Good News for us. You all have brought a dream of mine to reality. For that, I'm truly grateful. Lisa M. Clark, my editor, thank you for fine tuning my writing and bringing your skilled precision to bear on this book. You made this process easy for me and made the book better with your deep knowledge of words, sentence structure, and flow of thought. It's an honor to work with you. Last, but certainly not the least, I'd be remiss if I did not thank my fans and supporters who have gone on this journey with me, allowing yourself to consider Christianity according to its ancient roots as preserved through Lutheran thought. I know it was a bit frightening, but many of you have expressed gratitude and others have taken the same path as I have. For that, I am grateful.